ACCLAIM FOR
THREE RULES OF MARRIAGE

"The *Three Rules of Marriage* is necessary for an intimate and committed marriage that wants to thrive. Learning to live with and honor the "vows" of marriage with integrity and love takes investing in walking a path together. This book can show you how...Bill & Elena are walking the path."

—Bettie Spruill, CEO of *Ideal Coaching Global*

"Great insight and three easy-to-use steps to facilitate long term relationships. Thank you Carmodys, for sharing your pragmatic and insightful tools that will forever be a part of my romantic relationship."

—Tonya O. Parris, Co-Founder of ALTRU Center and CEO of Parris Group, Inc

"The *Three Rules of Marriage* effectively simplifies what is so often a complex area for so many people: relationships. Not only do Bill and Elena give their personal experience and wisdom throughout the book but they offer so many incredible resources that design your relationship and marriage to win. If you want to create a blissful marriage then the *Three Rules of Marriage* is a definite tool that you want as part of your journey."

—Michael DeSanti, Trainer, Coach and Author of *New Man Emerging*

"The psychology behind the *Three Rules of Marriage* will make your relationship better, but not just with your spouse. Couples who follow these rules will model "fighting" fair, strong values of concern and gratitude for other people, and emotional self-regulation for their kids. These are critical skills for understanding and navigating any relationship successfully. I highly recommend this book."

—**Michael Harris,** MA, LP, SEP and Director of Counseling
Services, Indian Health Board of Minneapolis

"Reading the *Three Rules of Marriage* as a 40-year old single woman renews my hope that it is completely possible to have a blissful marriage. The exercises in the book, nudged me to take an honest inventory of how I have shown up in past romantic relationships. To be frank, I have been a championship belt level scorekeeper. Simply leaning into one of the three rules will has already had a profound impact on all of my relationships. I have found the exercises in as a great checklist for myself and any future partner. I am excited to share this work with my friends who are single, dating and married. We all deserve blissful and powerful relationships."

—**Keita H. Williams,** Coach, Founder and
Chief Strategist of *Success Bully*

"The *Three Rules of Marriage* by Bill and Elena Carmody is sure to be the GO-TO book for successful unions for decades to come! I was excited to NOT be reading, "just another relationship book." This is broken down in an easy, thought-provoking, practical guide and workbook for couples. If you are committed to having your relationship thrive, flourish, and be full of love and appreciation, this is the book for you. I loved both its depth and simplicity. I am now going to use this as a resource for my personal development training company and coaching practice."

—**Francine K. Rahe,** Master Transformational Trainer,
Coach, and Co-Founder of AMP Trainings

"I had the opportunity to be an early reader of the *Three Rules of Marriage* by Bill and Elena Carmody. I immediately began to implement the tools into my own relationship. I immediately saw a positive difference. These tools are powerful and effective. Don't miss this instructive and significant new standard for couples — that actually work!"

—**Chris Austin,** Co-Founder of AMP Trainings,
Transformational Trainer

"Bill Carmody is a fantastic storyteller and his latest book, the *Three Rules of Marriage* combines sage wisdom with easy to implement insights and advice. This book provides a blueprint for lasting love in your primary relationship. If you're looking to take your relationship to the next level, pick up this book. Once you start, you won't want to put it down."

—**Phillip Stutts,** Founder & CEO of *Win Big Media* and
Author of *Fire Them Now: The 7 Lies Digital Marketers Sell...
and the Truth about Political Strategies That Help Businesses Win*

"So much joy and happiness can come from your primary relationship — especially when you give it the kind of love and support it deserves. In the *Three Rules of Marriage*, Bill and Elena Carmody show us what it takes to build and grow the kind of relationship we want today and for decades to come. It's fun to read and powerful to implement."

—**Kris Delgado,** Conscious Influencer and
Transformational Trainer

"The *Three Rules of Marriage* speaks to one of the great factors behind success of any kind: the transformative power of relationships. The focal point of this book is marriage as seen through the eyes and experiences of its husband and wife co-authors, Bill and Elena

Carmody. Together, they outline a roadmap to a better marriage. But in the process, they also outline a roadmap to a better, richer, fuller life based on the quality of your relationships and your willingness to invest in them. If you're seeking improvement in your marriage, buy and read this book. If you're seeking an improved life and way of living, buy and read this book. It's a short, practical, and personal book with clear pay offs along the way. By the way, Rule #2 is worth the price of admission alone."

—**Douglass H Hatcher,** Co-founder and President of
Communicate 4IMPACT; Co-Author of *Win With Decency*

"What a fantastic book!! The *Three Rules of Marriage* is packed with wisdom, inspiration and love. At this time more than ever, couples need to know this! Give yourself, your partner and family the gift of this great read."

—**Paula Jennings,** Founder & CEO of *Anam Evolution* and
former COO Americas CB&S Finance, *Deutsche Bank*

"In a Harvard Study of adult development, one of the most extensive and enduring studies of health and human happiness, the single most important factor at age 50 determining one's health at ages 80 and beyond was not their level of cholesterol, physical activity or type of diet that was being observed. The study determined that the single most important factor in determining health and happiness is the depth and quality of our relationships. In the *Three Rules of Marriage,* Bill & Elena Carmody create a context and a simple path forward to discover, learn and practice, simply and clearly, the techniques to arrive at a high-quality relationship. This book is an excellent resource for any individual or couple interested in learning how to take ownership and responsibility for the quality of their relationships."

—**Christopher Chen,** a licensed acupuncturist,
Founder & CEO of *Eastern Scholars Healing Arts*

"Your one-stop greatest thought-provoking culmination of best relationship practices grabs you instantly. The *Three Rules of Marriage,* by Bill & Elena Carmody, is shared through their keen lens to bring harmony, respect and true value in creating positive marriages. It's so much more than 3 rules! Together, they have captured the essence of many leading relationship experts and the impact on their marriage – highlighting Elena's parents 64-year marriage! Their stories are told through their voices based on (primarily Bill's) insightful viewpoints and their experiences are easily relatable. This book brings to life action steps you can immediately implement in your own life, with a solid background from Positive Psychology, Coaching skills and Positive Intelligence. Not just for married couples – for anyone who wants a long lasting, truly loving relationship!"

—**Ellen Nastir,** M.Ed., PCC, Owner/Founder of
Innovative Team Solutions and Co-Author of
When Divorce Crosses Your Mind: What Your Need to Know

"The *Three Rules of Marriage* is insightful and resourceful even for singles. Smart and simple laws to support an environment where relationships flourish."

—**@MarkMeyerHere,** star of *Baggage Battles* TV Show
and Multimillion Dollar eCommerce Rockstar

We dedicate this book to every person
who seeks a primary relationship
that stands the test of time.

Know that you are
whole, perfect and complete
and that you deserve the loving
relationship of your dreams.

Life is better
when you share it
with someone you love.

THE THREE RULES
OF MARRIAGE

Bill & Elena Carmody

Halo
PUBLISHING
INTERNATIONAL

ISBN: 978-1-61244-822-0
Library of Congress Control Number: 2020903272

Printed in the United States of America

Halo Publishing International
8000 W Interstate 10
Suite 600
San Antonio, Texas 78230
www.halopublishing.com
contact@halopublishing.com

CONTENTS

IMPORTANT: READ THIS FIRST

There is a wealth of additional resources at ThreeRulesofMarriage.com including:

- Companion Workbook
- Blogs and Bonus Content
- Interviews and Podcasts
- Live Events
- Videos
- Online Seminars
- Individual and Group Coaching

This book is also available as a audio book on Audible.com. If you love this book and would like to share the first two chapters of this book for free, you may do so at ThreeRulesofMarriage.com.

Bill Carmody is available for coaching, training, interview requests, speaking engagements, content development and marketing mastery.

And, we'd love to know what you think about this book. After reading or listening to it, please leave your HONEST review on Amazon.com. Thank you!

This book is part of a series. See more at WholeLifeSeries.com.

WholeLifeSeries.com

INTRODUCTION: WHAT DOES THIS BOOK HAVE THAT OTHERS DON'T?

If you want to discover how to build a life-long blissful marriage and absorb all the insights and wisdom from decades of screw-ups, attending 12 seminars, reading 57 books and talking to over 120 relationship experts, then continue reading.

But first, let me introduce myself.

Hey my fabulous reader, this is Bill Carmody. I'm one of the two authors of this book. And since there are two of us, I thought it might help if you knew who was saying what in each chapter that you read.

I was 12 years old when my father asked my brother and me to sit down. My first reaction was, "Uh oh, what did we do?" Nervously, I looked at my brother who shared the same expression of confusion and concern on his face. It was never good when dad asked us to sit down. This was serious. There was a long pause as my father thought about what he was going to say.

Then he opened his mouth and said, "Your mother and I are getting a divorce."

Everything after that statement seemed to go in slow motion. For the first time, I noticed the feint sounds of my mother sobbing. I looked over at her and she was breathing shallowly with her left hand over her mouth. Her eyes were shut tight and her face was squished into an anguished pose of someone doing her best to keep it together.

"What is happening right now?" I asked myself in disbelief. I was in shock. I didn't think that this could happen to us. My brother who was 10 years old, leapt off the couch, dropped down to his knees and wrapped both of his arms around my father's legs. As tears ran down his face, he looked up at my father pleading with him, "Don't leave me daddy. Please don't leave!"

"Who will take care of our family when dad is gone?" I thought to myself. "How will we survive? Are we going to have to move?" The questions swirled around in my mind. I was having my first out of body experience. It was as if my perspective floated up above me and I was keenly aware of my mom sobbing, my brother's desperate pleas and my dad doing everything he could to keep it together. I felt disconnected and numb. I wanted to cry, but I felt empty inside. I was devoid of all feelings and emotions. I was dumbstruck.

Then it happened. I noticed the tears starting to run down my dad's cheeks.

"I'm sorry," my dad said. "I have to go." And with that, he gently, but firmly physically removed my brother from his legs and walked out the front door of our house. This was the moment when my whole life changed.

Divorce is hard on everyone.

For kids, it rips at the very fabric of safety, love and connection.

Even if I suspected that my mom and dad were having a few challenges, I never imagined that they would get divorced.

No one does. No one plans on getting divorced. The purpose of this book is to share what my wife Elena and I have learned so that you and any children you have (or decide to have) can avoid experiencing this traumatic event.

ABOUT THIS BOOK

I am the first to admit that there are so many fantastic books already written about love and marriage, and so it begs a few legitimate questions such as:

1. What does this book have that the others don't?

2. What makes either of the authors an "authority" on the subject?

3. Why should I listen to either of you?

Think of this book like a buffet of insights and wisdom taken from decades of screw-ups, reading lots of books and talking to many experts. At the end of all of it, the insights I'm about to share have worked out really well for me.

In addition to building a 20-year blissful marriage (at the time of this writing), I also built and exited two multi-million dollar marketing agencies; completed a 140.6-mile Ironman; a 70.3 mile half Ironman; delivered a TEDx talk on storytelling; achieved a 4th-degree black belt; and interviewed such powerhouses as Sir Richard Branson, Tony Robbins, Seth Godin and Malcolm Gladwell. None of that matters in the slightest unless you know how much I care, or as Teddy Roosevelt so eloquently put it, "No one cares how much you know until they know how much you care." Despite my achievements, I value love and connection over significance.

What I care most about is living a blissful and legendary life. Sure, it includes all the things I mentioned, but none of them would have brought me joy without the ability to share them with the love of my life, Elena Knies Carmody – who is the co-author of this book – and our two amazing boys, Will (15 years old) and Ryan (12 years old).

MEET THE REAL AUTHORITY

Now my wife, Elena, on the other hand, is the real authority in all of this.

The trouble is, while I LOVE to write, she's less of a fan, preferring instead to read books, listen to podcasts and belly dance. Yup, you read that right.

She's been belly dancing for about as long as we've been married. And as beautiful as she looks from the stage, my favorite insight came from her late teacher Eli , who liked to remind her audience, "No one owns the art of belly dancing. The teachers are simply the stewards of our generation so that we may pass it down to the next generation."

And that, my friends, is …

WHAT THIS BOOK IS ABOUT

Sure, you can spend the next two decades fumbling around trying to figure out love and how to create a blissful marriage, or you can go straight to the source. That's NOT me (or Elena) by the way. It's actually YOU. You are the source of the most epic and blissful relationships of your life – including marriage. What I found, however, is that having some foundational rules really helps direct your focus, language and therefore your outcome.

So, let's get the answer to the most obvious questions you probably have.

1. What does this book have that the others don't?

First, the wisdom of Richard and Connie Knies, Elena's parents. When I first met them, I was shocked to see that not only were they married for over 40 years, but blissfully so. I mean it. They were still patting each other on the butt like two newlyweds on their honeymoon. I never once witnessed them get angry at each other, and when one spoke, the other listened – I mean they were fully present and hung on every word the other spoke.

Richard and Connie Knies became my North Star of the kind of marriage I wanted to have in my life. Later in the book, I'll tell you the story of how I came to learn the Three Rules of Marriage, but suffice to say, they were handed down to me by my father-in-law when I asked him how he was so happy in his marriage.

This book offers NO advice. That's right. Both Elena and I believe you were born whole, perfect and complete. We understand you've had many painful experiences that shaped your view of love, relationships and marriage. Rather than "being right" about what we've done, we are here to share a well-worn path of success we both were fortunate to discover from Elena's parents. The rules shared with us have supported us in building a blissful marriage both of us came to rely on. Unlike many of our friends who we hear complain about how much "work" their marriage is, more often than not, we tend to fill each other up and go out of our way to support each other. In other words, our marriage makes the rest of our crazy lives SO much easier, happier and joyful. If our lessons can support you, then they are well worth writing down and sharing with you. Wouldn't you agree with that assessment?

2. What makes either of the authors an "authority" on the subject?

Let's cut to the chase. Most "experts" are full of themselves, aren't they? What I find fascinating are all the love and relationship "experts" who are themselves single, divorced or unhappy in their marriages. If you were trying to lose weight, would you honestly listen to someone who is obese? Of course not. You want a drill-sergeant personal trainer who has a rock hard body and willing to kick your ass for your own good.

What Elena and I offer is sound, practical insights that have stood the test of time. These insights were both handed down to us by Elena's parents and time-tested over nearly two decades of our own marriage, which continues to grow and prosper.

I personally attended some of the most powerful and incredible transformation seminars currently available. At the end, I'll speak about my experiences in more depth. As a highlight here, know that I completed every Tony Robbins course currently available, Parts 1, 2 & 3 of Altru Center (an offspring of the original EST program from the 70s), Marcia Martin, and a significant financial investment in personal development training – all boiled down into easily understandable chunks in this book.

In terms of certifications, at the time of this writing, I am a Professional Certified Coach (PCC) level with the International Coaching Federation (ICF) and Elena is a Certified Leadership

Coach and an Associated Certified Coach (ACC) level with the ICF. So while neither of us are Marriage Counselors, we both are well-qualified coaches who support the various needs of our clients – including marriage coaching.

Elena and I are both extremely well read, which means we have sifted through countless insights, nuggets and bullshit from the love experts. Elena has a premium podcast subscription to the Savage Lovecast and shares all sorts of sex and relationship challenges that she finds fascinating, amusing or both.

And most of all, *Elena and I have NO attachment to being right about any of it.* Despite all of this knowledge and our collective wisdom, what is most true is that none of it matters if it doesn't work for you. So why write a book at all?

It's simple. This book is our gift to the world. Having already published a book with Wiley, I'm clear on the fact that most authors don't make much money publishing their book. We want to share our insights with as many people as possible who could benefit from them. By choosing independent publishing, we kept the cost as low as humanly possible. Today, information wants to be "free" and information wants to be "expensive." When you spend $10k for a relationship training, that's expensive information. When you download a book (or have it sent to your house) for a few bucks, then that information wants to be "free."

To that end, after reading this book you'll likely think of some friends and family members who could use the insights you gleaned . We encourage you to share the knowledge you're about to acquire. After all, the more people who are living in a blissful marriage, the better the world will be. Think about it. Blissful people don't seek out ways to hurt other people. The people who become suicide bombers and mass shooters are in some serious pain and lacking love in their life. Wouldn't it be great if, together, we could create a world that is loving, inspirational, compassionate and free? I believe world peace is possible in our lifetime. And the way to achieve it is through deeper love and connection. That starts at home. When my home is full of love and compassion, I am inspired to be my best self and feel free to take on anything I desire. That's what I want for you too.

Be honest with yourself. If all of this sounds like utter bullshit, then it's time to put this book down and do something else with your time. Whoever recommended or gave you this book saw a new possibility for you in your life. While the contents of this book clearly resonated with the person who gave it to you, there's no guarantee it will resonate with you.

This first chapter is intended to set you up for success; to get you excited to read on and consider a new possibility in your love, your relationships and your marriage. And it isn't for everyone. Another favorite quote of mine is, "When the student is ready, the master appears." While there's some dispute as to who actually coined this phrase, it's largely attributed to Buddha. Regardless of who said it first, the key concept is about readiness for change. Only when a person is ready for change in their life will they seek out wisdom from those who have gone before them.

If you know you're ready for some alternative perspectives in your life, then read on. While this book was specifically written to support married people, the concepts will easily translate into any relationship you would like to deepen in your life. The same three rules work just as well to deepen a friendship as they do to strengthen the bond with your lover. In fact, it's the people you love most (platonically or romantically) that reflect your own happiness and joy in life. The most pain I ever experienced came from "being hurt" by the people closest to me – a business partner who took advantage of me, a girlfriend who cheated on me, etc.

I later learned from some powerful teachers that I'm responsible and grateful for all of it. Some of the biggest pain points in my life provided some of the most powerful and lasting lessons and made me who I am today. If you've made it to this sentence, then clearly you're ready for some new ideas to consider, and I applaud your focus and commitment to taking your relationships to the next level. This book was written for you and I trust that it will support you in the many ways these insights have supported Elena and me throughout the years.

THREE SIDES TO EVERY STORY:
HIS, HERS AND THE TRUTH

B ill here.

Interesting fact.

"*III Sides To Every Story* (pronounced Three Sides To Every Story) is the third album by the Boston funk-metal band Extreme, released in 1992. It was the follow-up to the very successful *Pornograffitti* album."[1] I enjoyed the music during my college years and the idea came to me when I decided to write this book.

In Extreme's album, they clearly explain the three sides as "mine, yours and the truth." As I was talking to Elena about writing this book, I discovered some powerful nuances that we both took away from the three rules we're about to share. Upon deeper reflection, it dawned on me that both Elena and I "heard" the wisdom passed onto us with our personal filters and therefore, took away some powerful distinctions for ourselves.

Rather than attempting to wrestle these nuances to the ground in an "I'm right, you're wrong" sort of way, I invited her to write her own version of what she has picked up so you, the powerful reader, can see that even in the sharing of the three rules, there is, in fact, nuance and interpretation. Ultimately, Elena and I did exactly what I trust you will do – try on that which will serve you and let go of anything that doesn't. We certainly did, and it really worked for us.

To that end, this book was written from two unique perspectives. In the "He Said" section, I get to share my story of what I learned and how I've applied these lessons in the day-to-day building and growth of our marriage. In the "She Said" section, Elena shares her story of what she learned and how she's applied these powerful insights in a manner that allowed our marriage to blossom.

And for the areas where we both adamantly agreed, we created a section called, "The Truth Is…" as a means to share what we see as universal truths that, together, we uncovered from our relationship and marriage partnership.

Take a moment to imagine what we set out to do together. How many couples do you personally know who love each other so much that they have a deep desire to share their experiences with anyone who can benefit from them? While I am proud that we accomplished writing this book together, I feel privileged to have a willing partner who appreciates what I enjoy doing and desires to do it with me – even if this is a stretch and not something she would go out of her way to do alone.

The act of writing and sharing this book is one of pure love. To be clear, neither Elena nor I expect this book to provide any meaningful financial support to our union. If it does, that's a happy bonus. Why we decided to do this is out of a deep desire to contribute to YOU. By picking up and reading this book, you are telling us a lot about yourself. Specifically, that you:

1. Desire to create one or more powerful relationships in your life.

2. See the possibility of a happy, and at times, blissful marriage.

3. Desire to dig into what's possible.

4. Are willing to do whatever it takes to achieve a blissful marriage.

5. Are open to new possibilities and ways of being that will support you in achieving these outcomes.

It is because of these desires in you that we took the time to write this book. We are so excited to share what we learned. And the last thing we'd like to acknowledge before we do is a powerful quote from Teddy Roosevelt:

"Nobody cares how much you know until they know how much you care."

I've been blessed with an insatiable curiosity and deep desire for knowledge and wisdom. I spent the first 25 years of my career doing everything I could to share all the sources of knowledge I discovered. It wasn't until the last five years that I began to truly understand why some people were open to my sharing what I knew and others were not.

My request is that you hear me on this one. Before we begin this journey together, know that even if we've never met and you don't know anything about me, I truly do care about you. How can that be? I can say that authentically because I am certain we are all on an individual journey in this life, but what we share are universal desires for love and connection (among other things).

At the end of this book, I will share some additional resources with you that I trust will support your journey. I didn't write this book because I want to look good. Significance is not where I come from – at least, not anymore. This book comes from an authentic place of contribution. It is our gift to the world as a means to support the continued awakening of our planet. When there is more love and connection in the world than pain and suffering, we will achieve oneness.

I believe all things are possible and that we create our own realities. My vision for you is powerful. I hold you in the highest regard and support your continued growth and transformation. I am excited for a time when our paths cross (if they haven't already) and thank you for investing your time and resources into reading this book. Be well and read on!

HE SAID... BILL'S VERSION

According to the American Psychological Association, "about 40 to 50% of married couples in the United States divorce. The divorce rate for subsequent marriages is even higher."[2]

This book was written in an effort to support anyone who desires to be in a relationship that stands the test of time. While the principles of this book support the institution of marriage, they can be applied to any relationship you wish to deepen and cultivate in your life.

CHECK-IN: THE CURRENT STATE OF YOUR RELATIONSHIP

So let's get into it. Think of the current state of your relationship. If you were to rate it on a scale of 1 to 5, what number would you use? For clarity, I define the different levels of a relationship as:

1. Single / Not In a Relationship

2. Planning My Escape

3. Accepting (i.e. "It is what it is.")

4. Happy, Joyful and Desire More

5. Blissfully Married (i.e. "Am I dreaming? How is it possible to be this happy?")

If you're not currently at a Level 5 "blissful" relationship and you'd like to be (or you are, and desire to keep it there), then this book is for you. Now, before you read anything else, it's time to check-in with who's sharing all of these insights with you.

Throughout this book, I share stories about my marriage and relationship lessons in an effort to illustrate points I trust will support you in your relationship journey. For now, here are the most important facts about me that support why you might want to keep reading.

#1: My Parents Went Through a Divorce When I Was 12 Years Old. This means I lived through the trauma that comes when two people who loved each other chose to separate and then get divorced. It is my deep desire to have nobody experience the pain and expense of divorce – especially not the kids in the family (assuming there are or will be kids in your future).

#2: My Wife's Parents, Connie and Richard Knies, Have Enjoyed a Primarily Blissfully Marriage for Over 60 years. I marvel at this fact even as I write it. At the time of this writing, I'm 46 years old, and so my in-laws have been married more than 14 years longer than I've been alive (18 years longer to be exact). Clearly, they are doing something right. But it's not just time. These two beautiful souls act like newlyweds. Seriously! Coming up on 64 years into their relationship, they still look at each other as if they just recently fell in love, laughing, joking and a model of how I want to be when I'm 86 years old. My wife, Elena, shares a similar vision for our future.

#3: This Year, I Celebrate 20 Years of a Happy and Often Blissful Marriage. I acknowledge that 20 years is less than a third of what my in-laws have experienced. And I attribute my 20-year successful track record with the Three Rules of Marriage handed down to me from Richard Knies – the man who's been married for over 60 years. Not only have I embraced these rules, but I can see the causation between when I am out of one of these agreements with my wife and it helps me quickly get back into the blissful marriage I want. (More on that later).

#4: My Experience Is That My Grandparents Lived a Loveless Marriage. It's sad, but that is my experience of the marriage my grandparents had. Sometimes divorce is a much better option than staying together "for the kids" or "in the eyes of God." My grandparents were what Jim Gaffigan jokingly refers to as Shiite Catholics. There were the most extreme Catholics I ever met – going on pilgrimages, parading statues of the Virgin Mary around and doing everything a layperson could do to demonstrate their faith. Divorce, for my grandparents anyway, was off the table. In their belief system, they saw that in the eyes of God, they were married for life. So, they stuck it out and did the best they could. I rarely witnessed anything I would chalk up to as "love" for one another. By the time I came into the picture, I would characterize their marriage as civil and tolerating one another. I did not want that for myself.

#5: I Am One of the Only Males In My Family Who Has NOT Gotten Divorced. In fact, when I count my first cousins and stepbrothers, I'm very much in the minority. The divorce rate in my immediate family is higher than the 50% national average. I share this only because I am certain that *without* Richard Knies' Three Rules of Marriage, there was a much higher risk of me following the trend. These rules are simple, powerful and effective. Results don't lie. And, to be clear, my family members are *not* their results. I am fortunate to have some of the most loving and kind family members on the planet. When two amazing, loving and incredible souls get divorced, it's that much more painful for all who are close to them.

#6: Some of My Closest Friends Have Gone Through Divorce — it SUCKS! No one likes to talk about it, but when a divorce happens with two friends you've grown close to, there is often unspoken pressure to "pick a side" – especially in the first year or two when both of your friends are in pain and needing support. Bottom line, I've seen way too many people I deeply love and care about experience the trauma and massive financial consequence of divorce. I would love nothing more than to encourage divorce lawyers to find a new line of work because they experience a sharp decline in clientele.

It is my belief that these facts support my claim to have expertise in the areas I'm about to dive into. However, for the analyzer community who may desire more qualifications, you can head on over to my LinkedIn page (Linkedin.com/in/billcarmody/) to get the details on my 25-year career, public speaking and executive coaching certifications (and/or you can feel free to read my "About Bill Carmody" page in this book).

Enough About Me. Let's Talk About YOU and Your Primary Relationship

Before we continue, I invite you to download the companion workbook at ThreeRulesofMarriage.com (if you haven't already done so). This way, you can capture your insights as we go.

At the beginning of this chapter, I asked you to assess your current relationship. Remember? I asked you to think of the current state of your relationship. If you were to rate it on a scale of 1 to 5 what number would you give it? What number did you rate yourself in your current relationship? Find the one below and let's dig into this a bit further.

1. Single / Not In a Relationship

For this one, I'm assuming you actually want to be in a powerful primary relationship. I state that because for some people, being single is both a choice and a happy one. If that's you, then the value of the *Three Rules of Marriage* will come down to preparation for a possible day in the future when you make a different choice.

That said, if you are single, not in a relationship, and have a deep desire to change that, this section of the book is for you. The first question I will invite you to ask yourself is, *Why do I want to be in a relationship in the first place?* May feel obvious, but do yourself a favor and answer this question. Bonus points for taking the time to write down your answer so you can see it clearly.

I want to be in a relationship because _____

_____

_____

As Simon Sinek would tell you, "Start with Why." He wrote a whole book dedicated to this concept with the same title. Most of the time we focus on the WHAT (i.e. I need to be in a primary relationship) without ever stopping to examine why we want what we say we want. The biggest mistake I've witnessed couples make is finding someone who "completes" them. While this was a powerful moment in the Tom Cruise movie *Jerry Maguire*, I'm going to urge you to step out of that potential pitfall.

Any powerful and blissful relationship begins with two whole people. If you're looking for someone who fills a void you notice in yourself, there's a huge problem with that. The risk is creating a codependent relationship whereby one person needs the other person to feel whole. It's a beautiful concept to imagine some person out there has exactly what you need to feel complete – your missing puzzle piece as it were. However, that visual interlocking relationship where your partner fills in your gaps is destined to fail.

Being ready for a blissful relationship begins with working on you first. This is not about perfection.

Perfection is an illusion.

This is about getting real with yourself and taking a good hard look at what gets to be improved so what you bring to the party is a well-rounded individual seeking to attract another well-rounded individual.

It is from that space the two of you get to grow together. Having a solid foundation is an important first step to building an epic relationship. At the very least, acknowledging the areas you get to work on *before* entering into a primary relationship will ensure that you're taking responsibility for yourself rather than relying on someone else to fill in your gaps – that's a recipe for disaster.

Mindfulness of yourself will ensure an awareness of the areas where you're growing so that growth can continue to happen after you enter into a primary relationship.

Now, with all that said, you get to look at who you really want to attract into your life. The more specific you can be the better. For example, if we switched the conversation to money and you said, "I want more money in my life," that's not very specific. I could give you $1, and technically, that satisfies what you asked for. Contrast that to, "In the next 12 months, I will double my income in a profession that adds purpose and meaning to my life."

With that example, be as specific as you can be about who,

exactly, you are looking to attract into your life. Beyond gender, notice what is important to you. The more specific you choose to be here, the more obvious this person will be for you when the two of you bump into one another.

The person I want to attract into my life is: _____

_____

_____

It will be obvious to me that this is the person I've been looking for when I notice: _____

_____

_____

Next, let's look at the prices you're willing to pay in order to attract a primary relationship into your life and build a foundation for long-term success together. An important part of being in a relationship is about growing *together*. That means making sacrifices along the way to ensure the person you want in your life has clear evidence of just how much they mean to you.

Here's Where Many People Get It Wrong

We assume that the things important to *us* are the same things that are important to *them*, and that's rarely the case (and the essence of where most relationships fizzle).

In Dr. Gary Chapman's brilliant book, *The Five Love Languages,* he breaks down the fact that all of us have our own love language, and we expect the love of our life to fluently speak the same language as we do. Often, two people have very different love languages and therefore have different expectations coming into the relationship.

If you haven't already done so, head on over to www.5love languages.com/quizzes/ to discover which is your primary (and secondary) love language. By having a clear understanding of your love language, you'll know what to ask for from your partner in order to constantly feel loved.

Let me use an example here to illustrate this point. My primary love language is "words of affirmation." What that means is I feel love when Elena shares her words of appreciation with me. When she acknowledges me for my hard work and the things I do to support both her and our family, I feel loved. My mistake early in our relationship was thinking it was the same for her. It wasn't.

While my primary love language is "words of affirmation," I quickly discovered that my wife Elena feels loved via "acts of service." That is, when I wash dishes, make the bed, take out the trash, go grocery shopping, fix the gutters, mend anything that's broken and support her and our family, she really feels the love coming from me. We were lucky in that she intuitively acknowledged me for my "acts of service," which gave me the very thing I craved in our relationship.

When you enter into a new relationship, I urge you to be clear about your love language as well as that of your partner's. Otherwise, it's simple to talk past one another just like speaking two different languages. How far could a relationship grow if you spoke German and your spouse spoke Hindi? If I never did the acts of service that Elena saw as her primary love language, it wouldn't matter how much I told her I loved and appreciated her – she wouldn't be *seeing* that love manifested in acts of service (and would not believe the words I'm saying).

Similarly, even if I contributed daily all the acts of service Elena desired from me, if she didn't affirm the work, I would crave affirmation and eventually become resentful when I didn't receive it.

See how easily two people can inadvertently talk past one another? If you're finding that your relationships aren't making it past the early stages, there's an excellent chance the person you are looking to be in a relationship with has a different love language than you do. It may be as simple as getting clear on your partner's needs during the early stage of the relationship so you can create a foundation from which to grow.

2. Planning My Escape

I honestly don't know which one is worse – this phase of the relationship or the next one "Accepting" a relationship. When my father discovered he was no longer in love with my mom, he felt he had two choices. (1) Accept that he was in a loveless marriage, or (2) Plan his escape. There's always three or more options, which we'll dive into in the pages that follow. For now, let's take a good hard look at the option of Planning Your Escape. This was the direction my father ultimately chose when he decided it was time to separate and get a divorce.

These are just some questions that run through many people's minds when they are considering exiting a relationship. What happened? How did we end up like this? I don't even know this person. How could I be so blind to end up like this? By the time it goes to this phase, usually a lot of pain has been exchanged on both sides. Marriage counseling, albeit usually too late, is sought out by one or both partners. Where counseling could work, it is often met by strong resistance from the partner who is convinced counseling won't work, is a waste of money and won't change anything. What they are often NOT saying out loud and often thinking is, "I AM NOT THE PROBLEM. YOU ARE!" They would love their partner to get counseling so they can fix the obvious problems they have – there's nothing wrong with me.

Or, the person who wants to go to counseling is wondering if the therapist can "talk some sense" into my partner and help them see how wrong they are. Either way, neither approach is likely to be successful as marriage counseling isn't about tallying up all the points to see who's right and who's wrong – even if one or both parties secretly wish that it were.

In fact, if you're planning your escape right now, chances are you gave up hope a while ago that anything can or will ever change. That's the real bummer because once the desire to grow the relationship has been lost, it can be extremely difficult to get that spark back into the relationship. Pain, frustration, anger and even hatred replace the feelings of love, joy and happiness that attracted both of you into the relationship in the first place.

The planning of the escape is about minimizing the damage that will occur when exiting the relationship. Usually this is about money, kids, and/or saving face (i.e. "looking good"). And, at some level, it's about not hurting the person we once loved. Despite all the negativity that has occurred in the relationship, when it's time to move on, the choice still exists around how to exit – with love and integrity, or blow up the bridge that was once a deep and loving connection between you both.

It's helpful to know the opposite of love is not hatred; it is indifference. If you are full of rage, anger and pent-up feelings you still wish to express, know this comes from a place of love – even when it is mixed up with pain, frustration and anger. Anger, it turns out, is just love without all the information. It is often the need to be right, feel superior and/or justify how things have been that gets in the way of seeing the person for who they truly are and deeply understanding the love you still have for them.

If part of you still is open to discovering a path back to the loving relationship you once had, know this is possible – even when it seems highly unlikely. What is required is taking ownership of the ugly. You can't change the past. What you (and your partner) said or did is done, and there's nothing you can do about that. What can be done is to accept things as they are and see a different possibility; one where the pain is healed over time and a new chapter in the relationship can begin.

If you both choose a different way forward, know it is possible to repair the damage through a new vision for your relationship combined with committed actions that show your partner your commitment to a loving relationship—the very one you originally envisioned when the two of you chose to connect and be together. Simply put, the actions you took in the beginning of your relationship can bring you back to where you truly would prefer to be.

Take a moment to reflect on what you did in the beginning of your relationship. Did you bring gifts to one another? What drove the romance into the relationship? Be specific, what did you do then to court your partner? How did you celebrate your achievements? What would you do on your dates? How would you let your partner know how much you cared and wanted to be in the relationship?

When I began this relationship, I would _____

_____

_____

Now, notice when (and why) all of that stopped. Be honest with yourself here. Really go deep if you want to get to the heart of the matter.

The reason I stopped taking these actions and building romance into my relationship is because _____

_____

_____

Now take a second look at what you wrote down. Were you being truly honest with yourself? Are you willing to take on the full responsibility of your part in why the relationship began to deteriorate? If so, go one level deeper here and really acknowledge what happened.

If I'm being really honest with myself, the part I don't like to admit is _____

_____

_____

Seeing all of this, I acknowledge I can rebuild our relationship by _____

_____

_____

The actions I'm willing to take are _____

_____

_____

And I'm committed to taking these actions by_____
_____ (date)

If you desire to get back to the kind of relationship you originally envisioned, it will take more than words to get there. Your committed actions will need to reflect your renewed commitment to your partner. And it will take some time for your partner to acknowledge the changes you are making. At first, they will not be accepted or believed. Allow the time and space to process, heal and keep going.

It may take six to twelve months to repair the damage. There will come a tipping point when everything changes. Be patient, stay committed, and it will happen. You cannot change your partner. However, your partner will see the changes you've made in yourself, and that will shift the relationship.

If nothing else, these changes will improve how you feel about yourself, and you will know you have truly done everything possible to get back the relationship you once craved so deeply.

Having taken these steps to rebuild the relationship, you may find that despite your every effort, it's time to move on. Know that these efforts were not "wasted." Meaning that, in the moment of deciding to exit the relationship, you know you truly have done all you could do. By owning your ugly, you gave your partner permission to do the same and let go of the past. Even if that's not the way it worked out, there is a renewed sense of compassion. It will make the exiting of the relationship less painful and minimize the damage. Two people looking to hurt each other in exiting a relationship bring out a level of drama and negativity that ensures both parties receive the very hurt they desire to give the other person.

Only through owning your own part in the relationship's failure and having a deep desire to leave the relationship with the same level of love and empathy in which you entered, then can an exit be clean and the drama minimized. You get to choose just how easy or difficult exiting the relationship will be – for both of you.

One of my favorite insights from my work with Tony Robbins was a simple, yet profound insight he shared. "There's only two kinds of communication: (1) A loving response and (2) A cry for help." Often that cry for help sounds like, "FUCK YOU!" If you can avoid mistaking that cry for help as a verbal attack, you can get curious rather than choosing to feel insulted by the attack.

While you cannot control what your partner says or does, by staying level-headed and not taking personally the negative verbal jabs and insults expressed, your partner's negative energy will (eventually) run its course and the level-headed person you fell in love with will emerge.

Often, what happens instead is a drawn-out battle that looks a lot like a tennis match to an outside, unbiased party. One person lobs an insult over to their partner, who, in turn, catches that insult and returns it to its owner with equal and often more pointed insult with some extra anger as topspin. And the game continues until one person says the very thing that sets the other off, and there is a temporary feeling of "relief," which comes from a sense of "winning" an argument. When really, all you've done is set yourself up for the next serving up of insults for the next round, which is destined to repeat for the foreseeable future until one or both of you decide this game isn't worth playing, so it's time to walk away.

The alternative is to allow the insult to fall where it may. You are not required to "receive" what someone else sends your direction. In fact, by not taking any of it personally, the energy behind the attacks quickly runs out. Only by resisting the attack is energy given to it, and therefore, it is prolonged rather than minimized.

3. Accepting (i.e. "It is what it is.")

This is the stoic's point of view. A stoic is defined as "a person who can endure pain or hardship without showing their feelings or complaining."[3] Often the relationship ends up in the space when the feeling of duty and responsibility take over the love and passion that once defined the relationship. Staying together for a purpose such as (1) Raising Kids, (2) Religious Beliefs, (3) An Unplanned Pregnancy, (4) Keeping Up Appearances, and/or a whole host of other reasons.

The stoic's point of view is "the path to Eudaimonia (happiness) for humans is found in accepting the moment as it presents itself, by not allowing oneself to be controlled by the desire for pleasure or fear of pain, by using one's mind to understand the world and to do one's part in nature's plan, and by working together and treating others fairly and justly."[4] On paper, that may even sound appealing. It means your highs are never too high and your lows are never too low.

It also means the relationship while technically "functioning" is often devoid of passion and that deep sense of love. Both partners are certainly civil to each other as a relationship based on acceptance means neither side is actively looking to change the other. The very nature of acceptance comes from a place where the person you married turned out either to be who you thought they were or not, and either is ok (read: and there's no need to try to change them or the relationship).

There's certainly value in accepting your partner for who they are and appreciating what they bring to the party. The challenge comes from how acceptance shows up in the relationship. Acceptance, while devoid of explosive anger, is also devoid of deep emotions – high or low. Imagine two people who are taking the mental health drug, Prozac – typically prescribed to people diagnosed as bi-polar. What Prozac does is keeps a person "even" by removing the massive mood swings.

When you remove the emotion from a relationship, only logic is left. While that may sound great in theory, it's not what most people want in their primary relationship. It was Blaise Pascal who once said, "The heart has its reasons of which reason knows nothing." The passion in a relationship makes it exciting. Often, this passion can lead to explosive arguments when two extremely passionate people have very different views on a particular topic that is important to each of them. This can feel like a passion rollercoaster with extreme highs and lows as a couple learns how to argue. This is where the Three Rules of Marriage can come in handy. Ideally, we want to keep the passion while reigning in the conflicts, arguments and tensions that tend to be the flip side of a passionate relationship.

When the passion goes too far, however, there can be a subconscious desire to curb or even eliminate the passion, thereby leveling out the relationship. Unfortunately, when that passion is gone, what's left is a relationship based on a mutual understanding of what's more important. This is where staying together stops being about the love in the relationship itself and instead turns toward something else. Common variations on this theme include staying together for:

- The sake of the kids

- Financial reasons

- Religious reasons

- Keeping up appearances

- College and higher education goals

- Career focus and/or advancements

- And many other reasons that seem perfectly logical

If you find yourself in an accepting relationship, answer the following questions for a deeper dive into how you've ended up in this phase of your relationship.

The primary reason my partner / spouse and I are together is so _____

_____

_____

_____

If I don't change anything in my relationship right now, the future I see for us is that we will _____

_____

_____

_____

One thing I'd love to change in my relationship to make it even better would be _____

_____

_____

_____

If my partner and I were to separate, the thing I would miss the most would be _____

_____

_____

_____

In order to go really deep here, we get to acknowledge our relationship has been constructed around the story we tell ourselves. Think back about why you first decided to get into this relationship. And then, why you decided to stay in it even after some of the passion was no longer there in the relationship.

The reason I decided to get into this relationship in the first place was because _____

_____

_____

_____

Even when things got tough, I decided to stay in this relationship because _____

_____

_____

_____

To be clear, if you're happy being in an accepting relationship, it's likely you can stay put until one of three things happen. (1) The thing you and your partner were holding onto is resolved or no longer an important enough reason to stay together. (2) The relationship needs of your partner changes and more is desired. (3) Your relationship needs change, and you desire more out of the relationship.

One common divorce trigger I'm aware of is when the last kid goes off to college and the parents are suddenly empty nesters. When the role of "mom" and "dad" is no longer available, each partner's identity shifts. When what was previously a major part of the relationship (and a driving force behind staying together) is gone, both partners face a decision to stay together or separate. In fact, often the decision to separate happens well before the last child goes off to college (see "#2 Planning My Escape" above). If there is an apparent lack of love and a perceived partnership based on something other than love, the decision to separate feels just as logical when the goal is reached as staying together made sense in the drive toward that goal.

If you sense you're headed in that direction, you have an opportunity to take corrective measure now before it's too late. And even if you feel like it may already be too late, wouldn't it be worth it to do everything you can proactively before that time comes? If nothing else, this will allow you to let go knowing you did everything in your power to make a difference and change the relationship while you still had an opportunity to do so.

The good news is that you have the power to change this relationship and the odds are good that it is not too late. By simply coming from a place where you deeply desire to renew what you once had, you will begin to act differently and see a new possibility. As you move toward your renewed vision for your relationship, you'll experience a powerful shift that will ensure your relationship moves to the next level where you're happy, joyful and back to where it all began. The Three Rules of Marriage will help you get there, so please read on.

4. Happy, Joyful and Desire More

If you find yourself here in your relationship, I want to congratulate you. You have discovered ways to create happiness for yourself and your spouse. The joy you experience comes directly from the gratitude you have from your relationship. In this phase, you are taking nothing for granted. You see what is possible for your relationship. And while you love what you have, you know there is another level. The drive to push to this next level keeps your relationship fresh, exciting and full of growth and possibilities.

What will help you right now is establishing your foundation and recognizing the key drivers that you got you to this place. Let's capture some of that now so we can leverage these insights later as you move toward a truly blissful relationship.

I am most happy in my relationship when _____

_____

_____

_____

I experience joy in my relationship when _____

_____

_____

_____

I know my partner truly loves me because _____

_____

_____

_____

I experience joy and happiness from my partner when (s)he

_____

_____

_____

Again, congratulations for achieving this level in your relationship. And you know there's another level here. You can sense it. You know if you take any of the things you wrote down for granted, it would be easy to slip and find yourself in a relationship no longer filled with the joy and happiness you experience now (see previous section on "Accepting"). Or, worse yet, become agitated, frustrated and feeling stuck − so much that you begin fantasizing about leaving the relationship and what that might look like (see "Planning My Escape").

To keep what you have and grow it into the next level, you have many options in front of you. The number one tool is gratitude. Being grateful for the incredible relationship you're in means you never take it for granted. In fact, when things get difficult in your relationship, you need only reflect on why you chose to be in this relationship in the first place in order to stay grounded.

Gratitude has another powerful benefit. It turns out you can't simultaneously be both grateful and carry a negative emotion such as anger, frustration or hatred. As you reflect on the gratitude you have for the relationship, you're less likely to get angry at your partner. And, when you do get upset, being grateful for specific aspects of the relationship helps put the minor infraction or annoyance into proper perspective. That means most of the fights blow over and get resolved quickly. The more gratitude you have in your heart, the more loving you feel for the person you are in relationship with.

To help kick this off, take a moment to reflect on the three things you're most grateful for in your relationship today.

Three things I'm truly grateful for in my relationship today are

1. _____

2. _____

_____

3. _____

_____

It is SO much easier to reflect on what you're grateful for when you're in a positive state in your relationship. By acknowledging the three things you're grateful for, you set yourself up for a solid foundation from which to equalize (or "level set") when you find yourself frustrated or angry. Often, the trivial stuff can get us twisted up. At the moment, the issue feels big, but when we put it into proper perspective, it's usually pretty insignificant; especially when we're clear on the big things we are most grateful for in our relationship.

And just like that, you're already on your path to moving deeper into a Level 5, Blissful Marriage. Just by setting your intention to *have* a blissful marriage, and taking the time to be grateful for what you have, you're holding up your relationship as valuable and an important part of the life you desire. The next level is about deepening what you've already established. It's about focusing on how to build even more joy and happiness in the relationship. It's about celebrating the life you and your spouse are creating together. Really, it's about whatever you choose to make it. As long as you are clear on what you want and are willing to do whatever it takes to achieve that outcome, you will get there – and probably a lot sooner than you think.

The Three Rules of Marriage will support you in your journey. It's truly fabulous to have a solid foundation from which to build the kind of relationship you desire. So before we dive into what these three rules are, let's get clear about what a Level 5, Blissful Marriage truly means (and what it doesn't).

5. Blissfully Married (i.e. "Am I dreaming? How is it possible to be this happy?")

No bullshit. If you have experienced Marital Bliss, you are willing to work your ass off to keep the marriage at this level. And that's the thing – marital bliss doesn't just happen. It actually takes a lot of work, focus and attention. But, when you've experienced exactly what you want your relationship to be, none of that feels difficult. Let's make some clear-cut distinctions right now.

Marital Bliss is NOT...

- Getting Your Way

- Being Right

- Having / Being In Control

- Finding Someone Who "Completes You"

- A Sustained Period of Being Head Over Heels In Love

- Constant, Never-Ending Sexual Encounters

While Marital Bliss can certainly include some of these components, none of these elements are the end game. Getting your way may feel great at the moment, but often leads to a "win-lose" paradigm – as does always being right. When getting your way and being right are the outcomes you desire, the opposite of Marital Bliss happens. This is where the "Yes, Dear" shows up and the drive from a Level 4 "Happy and Joyful and Desire More" relationship begins to trend down to a Level 3 "Accepting" one. Rather than fighting, one of you ends up surrendering and just allowing the other to "be right" (even when he or she doesn't agree).

The same goes for that deep desire to be in control. A Blissful Marriage isn't about controlling your partner. If what you desire is someone who does whatever you say, then invest in Artificial Intelligence and a Sexbot – the technology is getting a lot better and before you know it, you'll have a robot that does whatever you want it to do. That's not about love—that's about power. Being in control is about having power over someone. Taken to its logical conclusion, this is where abusive relationships happen – both physical and emotional abuse. While playing with control in the bedroom can be fun (i.e. light and dark energy, dominant and submissive, etc.), a blissful relationship is built on mutual respect and admiration, not a deep desire to control the other person.

What's less obvious is the idea of finding someone who "completes you." Hearing Tom Cruise say that line in the movies may create a powerful flood of emotions, but this isn't the goal either. If you're aware of what you get to work on for yourself, that's a wonderful thing. The shortcut is not finding someone to do that work for you. The notion that there's someone out there who "completes you" carries with it the notion you are somehow broken and not whole. It's much better to see yourself as a work in progress rather than the notion you need someone else to fill a void you see in yourself. Even if that were true and you found the perfect person to fill that void, this would create a dependency relationship – one based on need rather than one based on love, mutual admiration and fulfillment.

And finally, that sustained period of being head over heels is neither realistic nor the foundation of marital bliss either.

Falling in love is an incredible feeling. And it's your feeling brain overpowering your logical brain. That is, the part of your brain that processes feeling and emotion is heightened when you fall in love and your logical brain takes a back seat. What can your partner do wrong when you first fall in love? NOTHING! That's because we forgive just about anything when we first fall in love. At some point, however, every relationship must transition from the early stage of falling in love to one of sustained growth and happiness. Even the early sex in the relationship is usually followed by balance where both partners desire and make time for that level of intimacy. The relationship is dynamic, which means it will most certainly ebb and flow rather than remain at a peak state in perpetuity.

Marital Bliss Is...

• A perpetual feeling that you're the lucky one in the relationship

• Knowing your partner enriches each moment you are together

• Being connected to the love of the universe through a single person

• Growing old with a partner who you are connected to mind, body and spirit

• A deep feeling of love for all while connected to the one who fills you up

• A spiritual connection (regardless of religious beliefs)

• The space between two people where everything is possible

• Sharing your life with someone who enriches your life in every way

• Feeling powerful beyond measure in part because of one person who sees you for all you are and all you are yet to become

• Knowing someone loves you completely – warts and all

I've come to realize the very work we put into our relationships delivers the bliss we seek out of the relationships. You've no doubt seen the bumper stickers that say, "Freedom Isn't Free." I see this statement as an acknowledgement of all the hard work, blood, sweat and tears our military deliver and sacrifice in order to create the freedom we enjoy.

The same is true with marital bliss. Modern conveniences have created some unrealistic expectations. When we can order just about anything with one click and have it arrive at our doorstep, we actively seek out convenience in every aspect of our lives. Why should a marriage be any different? And yet I find I do more things today I hated doing as a young adult because I know these efforts make my wife happy. The everyday efforts and contributions we make to our marriage are the very reason we have achieved the level of marital bliss we now enjoy on a regular basis.

So while seeking out and finding your partner is important, the contributions you make *after* your marriage make all the difference. The more effort you are willing to make in creating your ideal partnership, the more solid bliss you will experience in your marriage.

In his book, *Secrets of the Millionaire Mind,* T. Harv Eker said it this way, "If you are willing to do only what's easy, life will be hard. But if you are willing to do what's hard, life will be easy."[5] While he was referring to financial situations, I applied this insight to marriage as well. When I'm willing to have the difficult conversations and be raw and real with my wife, together we can get through any obstacle standing in our way. And we've had some grueling conversations in the nearly two decades we've been together. As a result, we've both made some significant sacrifices in order to create the partnership we both truly desire. Please do not mistake this for a dream. My wife and I created a blissful marriage because we were both willing to put in the work and create a relationship we both cherish. A dream is "out there" somewhere. Our efforts manifested exactly what we both wanted — even if we both had to adjust in order to achieve our desired outcome.

Marital bliss means never having to wear a mask. Think about that for a moment. How many people truly know you? How many people do you allow to see the real you — warts and all? Creating a false pretense is exhausting and unsustainable. And yet, go onto Facebook, Instagram, Twitter or any other social network of your choosing and see all the personas that have been created. How can we be true, authentic and real with our partner when half the time we're not actively being any of those things to ourselves?

Marital bliss is about demanding more from yourself long before demanding more from your partner. Marital bliss is less about *finding* "the perfect partner" and more about *being* that seemingly perfect person for your partner. As you show up as your best self, you create space for your partner to do the same. The real power and ultimately secret behind these 3 Rules of Marital Bliss, I discovered, is that at their core, they are about how you can be the best version of yourself so you can you create the relationship you desire.

Instead of imagining and designing your perfect partner, take a moment to check in with yourself and design the best version of yourself in order to attract a partner who challenges you to always be your best.

What I love most about myself is _____

_____

_____

The mask I wear the most is _____

_____

_____

_____

_____

For my partner to truly love me, warts and all, (s)he would need to know that I _____

_____

_____

_____

Most of us have a challenge answering that last one. That's because it requires a level of honesty with ourselves we don't enjoy. And that's the point. It's easy to be honest about the good things we see in ourselves. It's a lot harder to own your ugly. Being honest with yourself is about accepting yourself without judgment – much easier said than done. When you let go of the self-judgments, you can create a blissful marriage. This is because you accept yourself for who you truly are, and only then can someone else do the same.

These Three Rules of Marriage will support you in your journey. They have been a powerful foundation for a blissful 64-year marriage (my in-laws) and my 20-year marriage. Whenever I found myself out of alignment, I was able to refer back to one of the three rules, which gave me guidance and clarity around what needed to be done to get back to the marriage I truly desired.

How These Rules Were Passed Down (to Me)

Before I decided to ask Elena to marry me, I keyed into some of the best advice my father ever shared with me. Specifically, he said, "Son, before you ask someone to marry you, take a look at her parents – especially her mom. The proverbial apple doesn't fall far from the tree."

This was wonderful advice that I took to heart. When I first met Elena's parent, Connie and Richard Knies, they were the epitome of everything I ever wanted in a relationship. They were two amazing people, full of life, love and happiness. They treated each other with respect, and I never witnessed an unkind word uttered from either one of them about the other – not even in jest. Instead, I did catch each of them patting each other on the butt from time to time. It was as if they were newlyweds – only some 40 plus years into their marriage. I was in awe.

What I loved the most was how they looked at each other. I would catch Connie looking at her husband in a way that I almost felt like I could tell what she was thinking. If there was a thought bubble above her head (like in the comic books), I imagine it saying, "Look at this beautiful man. I am the luckiest person in the world. He is kind, thoughtful and amazing. I love this man so much." And then, out loud she would say something like, "Richard, dear, could you please..." and how could you not say yes to whatever she asked for when her tone and mannerisms were so on point?

And he was the mirror image of her. If Richard had a thought bubble over his head, I suspect it would say something like, "Wow. Am I the luckiest guy in the world or what? My wife is so amazing. She has such a great heart, she's incredibly talented and I love her to pieces." And then, out loud, he would say something like, "Connie, I want to thank you for this incredible meal. You're an amazing cook and this food is superb."

At first, I almost didn't believe it. It was like I had walked into a real-life episode of the black and white television show *Leave it to Beaver*. Eventually, I spent enough time with both of them to see that they did, in fact, get frustrated even with each other. They just showed it in the most loving and caring way I had ever witnessed. If Richard was upset, he'd say something like, "Come on, Connie, please hurry it along. We're going to be late." Yup. That was it. No personal attack. No making the other person wrong. Just stating the likely outcome of something not happening the way it probably should. Not so much anger behind the statement, but rather a sense of urgency.

When Connie wanted something from Richard he wasn't immediately into, she'd give him "the look." It was sweet as pie, and she'd just smile at him with that, "I know you're going to eventually see things my way, won't you dear?" It was both funny and sweet. And when Richard saw that look, he knew he'd be rethinking whatever original position he was holding when she gave him that look. After holding the gaze for a few moments, he nearly always caved and say, "Oh, all right" then chuckle to himself as if it was an inside joke in their marriage.

So I asked him, "Richard, what's your secret? I look at the way you and Connie treat each other, and I'm in awe of it. I've never witnessed two people so in love and so gentile to each other when you're not in agreement."

"It's simple, really. I love and respect Connie. If she thinks something different than I do, then I owe it to myself to hear her out. Her perspective really matters to me, so when she feels strongly about something, rather than 'dig in' with my belief system, I explore why she feels or thinks the way she does. Usually, it's something I haven't considered, and it changes my view. Very occasionally, I'll hear her out and still not agree with her, so I tell her what I think, and together, we'll work it out. It really helps that we both respect each other's opinion, so we're not going to dismiss something when either one of us disagrees with the other. Besides, we both follow a few rules for a happy marriage, and it's really worked for us."

My reaction was instant. "Hold on a second, let me get a pen." After a minute or so to grab a writing utensil and a piece of paper, I said, "Okay, continue. What are your rules for a blissful marriage?"

And what follows are the three rules he shared with me that day. So simple and so profound in their simplicity. And once implemented, they changed the way I viewed my partnership with my wife. Yes, I'm fully in love with my wife, and these rules supported me in ensuring that I never take for granted who she is and how lucky I am to be with her. Twenty years into our marriage, I'd ask her to marry me all over again with no hesitation.

Why These Rules Work

The day Richard shared these rules with me, I felt like I discovered the Rosetta Stone for marriage. They were simple, powerful and easy to implement right away. The simplicity makes them clear and definitive – either we're following each rule or we're not. When anything isn't working in my marriage, I just check in with myself – am I following the three rules? If I'm not happy or I'm feeling disconnected, it's usually because one or more of the rules have been broken, and I know it's on me to make it right. In addition to being simple, they are S.M.A.R.T. That is, they are specific, measurable, achievable, realistic and time-bound.

The paradox here is that we often think of the idea of freedom as being without rules or discipline. As the now famous former Navy Seal, Jocko Willink like to say, "Discipline = Freedom." Simply put, freedom doesn't exist without the discipline that goes right alongside it. These rules work because they are the very discipline necessary to have the freedom most people want in their marriage. Through the joyful rigor of these rules, you will experience the freedom of having a blissful marriage. Nevertheless, it's a learning process. Although I knew them, I got a lot of these rules wrong early in our marriage.

It's not about the number of times you stumble and fall. It's about how many times you choose to get up, dust yourself off and go again. These rules work because at their very core, they provide the foundation for the kind of relationship based on being fully present and in gratitude and appreciation for your partner. When you bring up the past or fail to acknowledge your partner for their contributions, it's easy to begin the process of taking your partner for granted. Rarely does a major rift in a marriage start as a major one – it usually begins as something small and irritating that goes unspoken and therefore grows and grows until a small issue feels like something enormous.

How to Implement These Rules in Your Daily Life

The best way to implement these rules would be the practice of mindfulness. Day to day, moment to moment what is your intention for your marriage? Who you choose to be and how you choose to show up is a massive reflection of how your relationship is with your spouse. These rules are a reminder of what it means to be in a loving, grateful and fully present relationship. When any of these three areas cease to be an important part of the relationship, the marriage struggles. Without love, the union becomes more like roommates than life partners. Without gratitude, it's easy to neglect the things that make the marriage powerful. And without presence, it's easy to live in the past and ignore what's happening right in front of you.

The power of these rules is that they allow you to check in with yourself to see what's working. Am I being fully present with my spouse? Am I acknowledging how much I appreciate my partner? When we are in conflict, am I focusing on how to solve this specific problem, or am I using it as a single example of a much larger source of contention? Perhaps one that isn't even "winnable" in the larger context?

As a daily practice, these rules support continued growth toward love, gratitude and presence in your marriage. They support you in opening up to new possibilities in your relationship and new ways of being that will ensure you are experiencing all your primary relationship has to offer. And there's always another level. As you go deeper in your relationship, you will discover the joy these new depths offer. While falling in love is a powerful euphoric feeling, so too is having a life partner who supports your continued growth. Having one person you get to spend your life with takes everything you do and accomplish to a whole new level. With each new level and depth of understanding comes increased clarity of vision. You enrich your life experiences by having someone to share them with.

First Rule:
The ONE Thing
You Can NOT Keep

When Richard shared this first rule of marriage, I let out a huge sigh of relief.

Before he explained the rule to me, I had a suspicion I knew where he was going with this one and why it was so important.

That said, my philosophy when anyone gives me advice is to listen with a beginner's mind of innocence—to hear the wisdom as if for the very first time so I may better apply this sage insight.

"The first rule of marriage is don't keep score," Mr. Knies told me.

"Whatever the argument is about, you're not allowed to drag up the past to prove your point. That means, whatever the disagreement or argument is about must be around what just happened so the issue can be addressed in the moment, and you both can move on."

This first rule rang to the core of my being.

How many times did I stack arguments in an effort to WIN?

Sound familiar?

As he explained this to me, I pictured my hall closet. I imagined keeping score was like putting small things that bothered me into the closet. Rather than living in the moment, I'd simply take notice and shove that thing into the closet. And I'd keep shoving things into the closet until one day, the closet couldn't hold any more, and with a tiny opening, it would all come crashing down on me as well as the person I love.

At the same time, I thought about all the relationship fights I'd ever been in up to getting engaged to Elena. It was never about the stupid thing that triggered me. It was about EVERYTHING else. A girlfriend may have been upset that I left an article of clothing on the floor, but the proverbial "pinch" did not equate to the proverbial "ouch."

Instead, what unleashed on me was every little thing I ever did wrong in the relationship.

All of it. Right there in that moment.

"You always do this! How many times do I tell you to pick up your socks and throw them in the hamper? That goes for the toilet seat too – you have to close it EVERY time you pee. You can't even put the toilet paper on the right way; assuming you replace the toilet paper at all. What am I, your maid? Seriously, pick up after yourself. You leave your dishes in the sink and expect the dish fairy to come and clean them for you. You never think about who cleans up after you. It's me! And I'm sick and tired of it…"

You get the picture.

Keeping score allows the offended party to stack the argument so there's no possible way to feel anything but defeated. Rather than having a calm and rational discussion about neatness and mutual respect, the argument quickly snowballs into "you're a terrible person and you should be ashamed of yourself."

It's a straight up attack and nothing productive ever comes of it.

So Why Do Most People Keep Score In the First Place?

We have been conditioned to "win" from a very young age.

Anytime we find ourselves in an argument, the desire to "be right" often overpowers our logic and reason.

If rational, we see the person we're arguing with is very important to us. And yet, the people we love the most are the ones who have the power to really push our buttons.

And when we feel triggered, our emotions have a tendency to take over.

We get enraged at the person who triggered us as it's SO much easier to blame someone for the way we're feeling rather than taking responsibility for our own actions. And so it begins.

The Blame Game.

YOU DID THIS TO ME! HOW DARE YOU! And then the amplification kicks in. "Not only that, but you also…" Or my personal favorite are the absolutes, "You ALWAYS do…" or "You NEVER do…" And so it goes.

Half the time, we don't even hear ourselves. Let me take this opportunity to own my ugly here. I had a manic-depressive girlfriend in college whom I loved dearly. The only thing I loved more than the manic sex we had is the passion that came before or afterwards. Damn! She was a hot mess, and I loved our passion rollercoaster. I'd say I didn't, but secretly, I knew the highs were never as high without the deep and low crashes. I didn't care, because the sex was amazing, and I could handle her ups and downs.

And when she wanted to fight verbally, I put on my mental sparring gear and was ready to go 10 rounds. She'd lash out at me, and I'd take whatever she said and figure out some way to one-up it. "Oh yeah, well…" and we went at it for hours—sometimes days. I didn't give a flying fuck what I said in the heat of the argument. And the knockout round was usually something particularly dark and painful for one of us.

You know how this ends because we've all said things we didn't mean in the heat of an argument. At some point, without even thinking, the nastiest thing launched out of my mouth. It was like my subconscious, knowing a future fight like this would happen, was secretly tucking away the most brutal thing it could grab onto and saved it for this moment. And then I spewed it.

The moment the words left my mouth, I instantly regretted saying it. But too late. Some things, you can't take back. The words cut her like I stabbed her in the heart, and her tears announced this was the final round of our verbal sparring match.

I won. But at what cost?

She was crushed.

The man she loved cut her to the quick, and she felt utterly alone.

The depression set in, and we might not talk for a full day – sometimes longer.

It truly sickens me to think there was a time in my life when I was like that. That I used my power of words for ill rather than good. Rather than building someone up, I used them to knock someone down – just to make myself feel better and "win" the argument. But it was never a win. The damage I did in the fight was far worse than whatever originally put us into the fight in the first place.

With each fight, I lost a little something of myself. And she did too.

Why would you ever want to be with a verbally abusive person (let alone physically abusive)?

The only answer I could come up with was low self-esteem and self-loathing. When you don't love yourself, those painful, vicious, attacking words ring true at some level because we're so damn hard on ourselves. We believe the lies because we feel less-than.

"Hello, Darkness, my old friend."

When someone attacks us, part of our defenses goes up, and another part takes the attack to heart.

We stayed together because of a familiarity and great sex.

When the passion runs red hot, those peak moments of pleasure can help you overlook the truth.

Maybe that's why people choose to stay in relationships they know they shouldn't be in. When stuck between a fear of loneliness and a bad relationship, many opt for the bad relationship and do their best to make it work. The trouble is you can't build a house on a weak foundation. If the mutual respect isn't there from the beginning and nurtured in order to allow it to grow, the feeling of brokenness keeps cropping up.

We can be hurt the most by the people closest to us, which is why it's so important to be mindful of who we let into our hearts from the start.

With the benefit of age, I can clearly see what an immature asshole I was in the relationship. When my heart was trampled on, rather than exiting the relationship, I focused on protecting myself by getting even and being right. I learned from the pain, but what I learned was how to win an argument and protect my feelings – that's not a formula for long-term success nor was it setting me up to win in love.

It was only with the benefit of time I could look objectively at my contribution to the pain and suffering in the relationship.

The answer to getting knocked down was not a deeper and crueler attack—that was what my ego desired. My higher self was already questioning my actions and searching for a better way.

The First Rule Combats This Ugliness and the Need to be Right

Not keeping score ensures that the focus is on a single issue at hand rather than the stacking of all the list of things you neglected to work through previously. If you're only allowed to address the single issue at hand, it means you get to let go of all the rest. What's in the past is just that – in the past. There's nothing your partner can do about mistakes they already made.

Not keeping score has other benefits as well. It means you have no emotional closet to throw any relationship baggage into in the first place. Think about that for a moment. How much lighter would you feel if you never had to carry around any emotional baggage? The concept of not keeping score goes well beyond reducing the number and length of the arguments you have – it sets you free.

When in alignment with this rule, it forces you to live in the moment. By not being allowed to hold on to the past, it forces you to deal with whatever is happening in the here and now. If you choose not to "get into it" with your partner, then the only other option is to let it go and never bring it up again.

Given that understanding, you get to answer a powerful question, "How important is this issue?" Remember the book, *Don't Sweat the Small Stuff?* Nearly all of it is small stuff, yet we spend way too much time keeping track of the nonsense. If something is bothering you, you get to check in with yourself and determine if you and your partner need to discuss it, or if you can let it go.

Initially, the temptation may be to bring it all forward and discuss it. That gets old really fast, and you begin to separate small irritants with the foundational issues that are important to you.

Hard Conversations, Easy Life

Earlier, I referenced T. Harv Eker's *Secrets of the Millionaire Mind.* His quote sticks with me, and I apply it in everyday life – not just when it comes to money and finance. "If you are willing to do only what's easy, life will be hard. But if you are willing to do what's hard, life will be easy." In context, when you are willing to have the often-difficult conversations, your life will be easy. However, when you're only willing to have the easy conversations, your life will be hard.

To me, that's the essence of effective communication. Not keeping score essentially forces you to have the tough conversations since you're not allowed to push them into the closet and save them for later. And the harder the conversation, the easier your life will be after the conversation happens.

The opposite is also true. How do you have easy conversations? Simple. You avoid saying what needs to be said. The reason easy conversations are easy is that there's an avoidance of all that is difficult to say. This is also where triangulation happens. Rather than speaking directly to your partner, you talk *about* your partner to other people. This is especially painful when what is shared is deeply personal and a real problem you'd like to solve. Inevitably, rather than handling the problem, we get the consolation prize: sympathy and advice.

So what ends up happening is that the problem gets bigger the longer it doesn't get dealt with. The hard conversation gets even harder, and the resistance to having the conversation grows and grows until it's no longer a conversation – it's an attack. The person on the receiving side of the attack does what anyone would do—defend against the attack, which shows up in the form of deflection and redirection. This is where the rule of not keeping score gets broken. When you're desperate to get off the hot seat, it's easy to pull out that list of all the things you'd like to change in the relationship and rather than dealing with the problem at hand, use this as an opportunity to air all your grievances.

What happens? Pain. Little is accomplished. Neither person feels resolution of the argument. And both are angry at each other. Does this sound like a blissful marriage to you? It may be passionate and the makeup sex may be fantastic, but it's not a winning formula for a blissful marriage. The alternative is a deep sense of gratitude and a willingness to get out of your comfort zone and grow.

When Your Partner Pushes Your Buttons, Thank Them!

If everything in your life was "perfect," you'd be bored out of your skull. That dream we've been chasing since we were kids is an illusion because perfection itself is an illusion. There is no perfect because perfection, by definition, can never be achieved. So let's stop chasing the illusion and get real. Happiness comes from the pursuit, not the achievement. That's what was written in the United States Constitution, "Life, Liberty and the *pursuit* of Happiness." That word makes all the difference.

We're all on our own journey in life. According to Ray Dalio, in his book, *Principles*, happiness comes from the art of struggling well. Too much struggle and we feel overwhelmed and defeated. Not enough struggle and we're bored and unfulfilled. Happiness is about finding that balance in your life where there's enough struggle so you feel challenged in your life, but not so much you feel helpless.

When I was studying to become an EE Dan (i.e., second-degree black belt), my master instructor, the late Mark Balaban, pulled me aside and said, "When someone pushes your buttons, you should thank them."

I looked at him with wide eyes and a confused look.

He could see that I didn't get it, so he continued. "You shouldn't have any buttons to push. So when someone pushes your buttons, you should thank them because now you know you have something you get to work on."

That insight really landed with me. In the don't-keep-score context, it means that rather than getting angry when your partner pushes your buttons, give yourself a time out and reflect on how it is that something so trivial can get you so upset. Awareness of a problem is the first step to solving it. This is why thanking your partner is so important. They are showing you where you get to work on yourself, and it is truly a gift.

Here's the secret: *it's never them, it's always you.* Your experience is just that. YOUR experience. When you feel triggered, it's your feelings. The event, whatever it was, was just the event. The emotion comes from the meaning you give the event. Being triggered is your body's way to alert you that something is off. Are you listening, noticing and learning from what's coming up for you? Or do you choose to blame someone for that uncomfortable feeling? Blaming someone else is simple. Working on improving yourself is much rougher but worth the effort.

How NOT to Keep Score

It begins with mindfulness. What do you do when you get irritated, frustrated and out of sorts? Do you pull back or lean into the issue? When you find yourself avoiding something, stop and question why. At the very least, notice any unwillingness to tackle a problem when it arises. As one of my mentors, Tony Robbins, likes to say, "What resists, persists." What we avoid continues to show up in our lives until we deal with it. Not dealing with something means you're putting it off and shoving it into a proverbial closet to deal with later.

Next, resist the temptation to amplify. The trap of, "you always do this" is the multiplier effect you're looking to avoid. Before getting into it, take a moment to check in with yourself. While you feel compelled to express how you feel, how can you do it in a loving, caring way that supports the continued growth in your relationship? Will this conversation bring you closer to the relationship of your dreams, or further away from it?

Sometimes, the best place to start is with the intention of letting go. If your proverbial closet is already full of the things you are upset with your partner about, then perhaps it's time to clean out that closet so it's empty. Think about that for a minute. What would it feel like if you always started with a clean slate? That alone is worth the price of admission. How exhausting it is carrying around the past wherever we go. How can we ever be fully present when lurking inside our closet are memories of all the things someone did to us in the past? How can we live in the present moment when we choose not to let go of the past?

Perhaps an exercise will help you here. What are the top five (or more) unresolved issues you immediately think of when you get into an argument with your partner?

The top five things I would like to stop holding onto with my partner are

1. _____

_____

2. _____

_____

3. _____

_____

4. _____

_____

5. _____

_____

Are those the top five, or just the first five that came to your mind? If you had space for another five, would you struggle to complete the list or look for more room to keep going? Notice this. Part of mindfulness is about being real and honest with yourself.

Moving toward a new future begins with being straight up honest about where you are right now. Only with that honesty can you truly let go and be clear of the past. The last chapter of this book, "So What, Now What" provides a number of resources to help clear out your emotional closet so you have a clean slate.

This simple rule is profound in its application.

By not keeping score, you are committed to living in the moment and working on whatever comes up for you. Or, if you choose not to work on it, you are committed to letting it go and not holding onto it.

When you truly align to this rule alone, you will find yourself living in the present and letting go of the past. Whatever issues come up in your marriage, you can choose to deal with them as they happen or choose to let go of the issue altogether. Either way, you are at choice and in control of your happiness.

Building a blissful marriage begins with being fully present, honest and open with each other. Not keeping score helps ensure that you're focused on the present moment in your marriage and not dredging up the past in order to win arguments or feel superior.

Second Rule:
The Most Important Thing
To Say To Your Partner
(And It's NOT "I love you.")

The second rule: "It's more important to say I appreciate you, than I love you."

Now this one blew my mind when it was shared with me. I really didn't get it at first.

Perplexed, I thought, "How can this be? Isn't love more powerful than appreciation?" So I asked for clarification.

"Appreciation is specific while love is general," Mr. Knies shared. "Look, you're going to spend more time doing dishes than you are having sex. Couples begin to drift apart when they no longer feel appreciated. Imagine you and your wife were just in a fight, and then she says to you, 'I love you.' Now it's easy to dismiss that as something you're supposed to say. However, when she says, 'Thank you for taking out the trash,' it's harder to dismiss. She genuinely appreciates what you did, and it's much easier to reconnect in the relationship."

Damn. I had been doing it all wrong. I was certain love was

the most powerful word to use. It took me months to work up the courage to say, "I love you," and Elena didn't immediately say it back.

Instead, she said, "Give me some time. I'm getting there." So when she finally looked me in the eyes and told me, "I love you," I knew it was genuine, that she searched her feelings and was being 100% authentic with me.

As a man, telling someone I loved that I actually loved them out loud was one of the most vulnerable things I could imagine. And yet, here was my father-in-law telling me it's more important to say I appreciate you than I love you. This was a game-changer for me. This rule was like that scene in the movie *The Matrix* when Neo sees the code underneath the world, and he is no longer "attached" to The Matrix.

I Appreciate You

At first, I felt awkward saying this all the time. It was strange and foreign for me. I grew up in a household where my mom just did everything, and I never saw anyone thank her. It just was what it was. I never stopped to think about the work that went into washing all those dishes, taking out the trash, mopping, sweeping, vacuuming, and all the other household chores.

It wasn't until I went off to college and had to do all of that stuff myself that I genuinely missed having my mom around to make me meals, do the shopping and clean up after me. She never once complained about doing any of it. My assumption (at the time) was that this was the role of "mom." That is, moms did all this work and didn't complain about it because it was the job they took on.

How naïve I was. To think anyone genuinely loves doing laundry, going to the grocery store or taking out the trash. We do those things because they need doing — not because we enjoy doing them.

I distinctly remember the first time I was living with roommates who all felt the same as me. We went out of our way to buy disposable, frozen microwave entrees so we had to neither cook nor do dishes. We zapped our food, ate it and then threw away the container, never giving a second thought to the higher price we paid for convenience nor the negative environmental impact or how bad for us this food was we were putting into our bodies.

As I thought about the biggest fights I had with my college roommates, it usually began with dirty dishes in the sink, the garbage overflowing or a disgusting bathroom that required attention. It was so obvious, looking back on it. These were thankless jobs. You only notice the trash when it's full or the dirty dishes when they pile up and no clean ones are left.

Appreciation is about bringing forward the acknowledgement for the otherwise thankless jobs in the marriage. When we're dating, there are all these fantasies about how life is going to be when you're married. For me, it was having a chef in the kitchen, a best friend to play with, and a sexually adventurous partner in the bedroom to satisfy all my sexual fantasies. Oh yeah, and an incredible mother for my children, who also happens to work making a ton of money and somehow finds time to clean up so our house is presentable when we have friends over for parties.

Now if only I can find the right form on Match.com to submit these job requirements, and I can find the perfect wife. That may seem laughable, but this is what many people are searching for: The

Perfect Partner. He/she doesn't exist! And if he/she did exist, do you have your act together in such a way as to attract this perfect mate? Rather than searching externally for someone who satisfies all of these ideals, this is a perfect opportunity to check in with yourself and take a hard look at what you bring to the party. Are you already the mirror opposite of what you seek?

For me, that would mean taking a hard look at personal cooking skills, the recreational activities I enjoy, how giving I am as a sexual partner, how good of a father I am, my career growth, financial freedom and cleanliness in the household. There's actually a powerful way to do this.

Partnership Readiness Wheel

This is a coaching tool you can use to assess any aspect of your life. To have a deeper appreciation for your spouse, it's great to take a self-assessment of where you are in your own journey first. Often times, we look to others to satisfy the things we're not happy with about ourselves.

So take a moment to review the wheel below. I've started with some of the more common categories you might want to look at. However, if one of them isn't important to you, feel free to cross it out and write something else that is more important. I've also purposely left one area blank so you can fill in something that is really important to have in your life.

Now, give yourself a rating from 1 to 10 in each area of the wheel. So, for example, if you can't cook worth a damn, find dirty laundry all over the floor and your bathroom is so disgusting you'd be embarrassed to have someone come over to your house, then give yourself a low score (1-3) for "Domestic Skills". Conversely, if you're a neat freak who borders on Obsessive-Compulsive Disorder (OCD) and your cooking is so good people often request recipes and recommend you enter food competitions, then give yourself a high score (8-10).

Life Mastery Wheel: *In order to live you best life (or remain living one), let's do an honest self-assessment on where we are:*

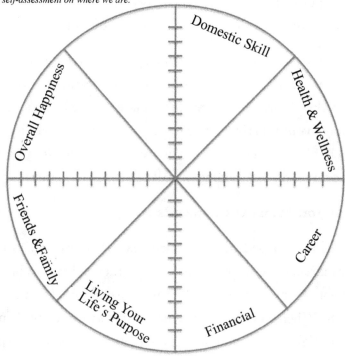

I've combined "Health & Wellness" to include physical appearance, so if you have a rock-hard body and Hollywood is dying to cast you for an upcoming superhero movie, then give yourself a high score (8-10). If your ass never leaves a couch, bed, driver's seat or office chair except when going to the all you can eat buffet, and you're wondering what the hell happened to that body you once had, then there's probably some room for improvement in the "Health & Wellness" area of your life.

Once you complete this exercise, step back and see what you notice. What areas of your life are you committed to improving? How will improving this area of your life support your deep appreciation for your spouse or support you in attracting the partner you desire in your life right now? Think about it. As you work on yourself, you become more attractive to your current (or future) spouse. And, as you put in the hard work, you become much more aware and appreciative of your partner who is doing the same thing.

Rather than seeking to find the perfect partner who has their shit together, I invite you to BE the kind of partner who has their shit together. Doing the work will give you a vast appreciation for what goes into each aspect of your marriage. The more you take responsibility for these aspects of your marriage, the more you appreciate any, and all, support you receive from your spouse.

What You Focus On Expands

This rule helped me recognize that whatever you focus on in your marriage expands. What your partner is doing right is always available — and so are all the things you don't like and desire to change. When you choose to focus on what's working well and going exactly right in the marriage, you're going to see and experience more of those things on a regular basis.

The power of appreciation is twofold. First, you are actively seeking out all the things your partner is doing right. When you're angry with your partner, this takes some doing. Anger blinds us. Anger prevents us from seeing all the acts of love happening all around us because we are fixated on the one thing driving us crazy. And, when you stop and seek out all your partner is doing on your behalf, you see the larger context. What's driving you crazy may only be 1-2% of what your partner is contributing to the marriage.

Focus on the 98% they are doing right and allow your partner to know how much you appreciate them.

Secondly, when you begin with appreciation, your partner is much more open to receive feedback about the things you'd like to change in the relationship. Please don't think this is some sort of manipulation technique. That's not what I'm saying. I'm acknowledging that when you make several deposits in the relationship bank of appreciation, you will have permission to make a withdrawal when the time comes to share the opportunities for improvement in the marriage. Conversely, if all you ever tell your partner is what you want them to change, it's likely they will begin to tune you out, ignore your requests or counter with all the changes they would like to see in you.

The power of appreciation connects you and your spouse to the small things that make up a great deal of the relationship. The small stuff adds up over time. When what your spouse hears from you is how much you appreciate them, they feel good about themselves – and about you. They don't mind doing the mundane chores that need to be done when they are clear you not only notice the work they are putting into the relationship, you've actually taken the time to say something positive about what they have done.

Appreciation has great benefits for you as well. The only way to say authentically that you appreciate something your spouse did is to begin with gratitude. The more grateful you are toward your spouse, the more grateful you become in other areas of your life. *With an attitude of gratitude, you are unstoppable.* No one wants to be around a miserable person. Misery may love company, but who wants to be pulled down from a place of happiness? Instead, when people experience you as grateful and appreciative of all you have in your life, the people around you want to hang around and see what you're doing so they too can have more happiness and fulfillment in their life.

And the rabbit hole keeps going deeper. It turns out it's impossible to simultaneously hold anger and gratitude in your heart. Whichever emotion you feed gets stronger, so as you pile on your appreciation for your spouse, you too become happier and more content in a number of other areas in your life.

Ultimately, I have found that appreciation is the foundation for mindfulness. When people talk about wanting to bring more mindfulness into their lives, I ask them what three things they can be grateful for in this moment. For example, I am truly grateful for scheduling the time to write this book. I am grateful for my kids who are running around and playing – they are growing up fast, and I'm not sure how many more years we get to have them in our house as they near college age. And I'm grateful that while I was writing this paragraph, my wife was teaching my oldest son how to cook a healthier meal. Despite his lack of interest in this lesson, I know her diligent work will support my son's healthier eating for decades to come.

Now it's your turn. What are three things you can be grateful for right now if you choose to be? Are you truly grateful you have made time for yourself to read this book? Could you be grateful for the weather you are experiencing right now? How about the simple things like the air you are breathing or the clothes you are wearing? Speaking of clothes, could you be grateful you didn't have to make what you're wearing today? Can you give thanks for the person who made sure the clothes you are wearing passed a quality standard? You get the picture.

Things I'm Grateful For About My Spouse

Now let's drive this one home. Rule #2 is that it's more important to say, "I appreciate you," than "I love you." So let's do it. What are the five things you will tell your spouse you appreciate about him or her the next time you see him or her?

Five things I appreciate about my spouse include

1. _____

_____

2. _____

_____

3. _____

_____

4. _____

_____

5. _____

_____

Now make a plan to share these with your spouse. Remember, the more frequently you share how much you appreciate him or her, the more your gratitude will grow overall. Come up with fun ways to share your gratitude with your spouse.

This was such an important rule that my wife and I decided to share it with our children. Every Saturday is allowance day. Rather than handing out the money, we turned it into a family meeting. The kids get together with us and go around acknowledging each other. It may be something as simple as, "Ryan fed the cat even though it was my turn."

Occasionally, one of us has already welled up with gratitude and speaks deeply from the heart. "I would like to acknowledge Dad for working so hard. He makes all of this money so we can go on vacation and travel around the world. I'm so lucky to be part of this family." Or, "I want to acknowledge Mom for reading to us every night before we go to bed. You could have stopped a long time ago when we learned to read, but the fact that you do this every night is really cool. Thank you!"

How often does your 12-year-old son speak to their deep gratitude? If we hadn't set up this time to connect and be together, I don't know that it would have come up naturally. Just having a dedicated time each week has supported the loving bonds of our family. And it started with Elena and me modeling this for each other and our children.

"Hey honey, thank you for washing my pot. I was planning on cleaning that after my call, but you beat me to it. I appreciate you." Who said that? Both of us to each other at one point or another.

I used to keep score (in violation of Rule #1) with my post-college roommates when they didn't do their dishes. I was outraged by how they chose not to clean up after themselves and left dirty dishes for everyone else to deal with or work around.

Now, however, I don't even think twice. If there's a pot soaking in the sink and I have a few minutes to spare, I don't hesitate to wash it. I'll admit I've slipped on taking out the garbage, and I never miss an opportunity to thank Elena when she does it.

Can You Still Be Grateful and Appreciative When Upset?

Being authentically grateful and appreciative is harder to do and takes practice. When things are generally going well in the relationship, it's pretty easy to thank your partner for their acts of service. From laundry to putting the clean dishes away, when things are good, it takes just a little extra effort to stop and thank your spouse for the household chores.

When you're in the thick of a disagreement, however, it takes practice to be able to disconnect from the issue at hand and drop into your authentic gratitude. This is also called a pattern interrupt, and it can be hugely beneficial to the marriage. Let's say you just had a blow up and each of you disengaged from the argument to "cool off" before you say something you'll regret. As you walk into the bedroom, you notice your clothes neatly folded in the hamper on the bed. Notice what happens next. The ego side of your brain wants to make this part of whatever argument you just had. "Sure, she'll do the laundry, but if she spent half as much time doing [whatever the fight was about] as she does the laundry we'd be so much better off."

Or you can take a moment and laugh. Notice what nonsense the fight was to begin with. Here is the person you married. The person you love. The person who has become an extension of yourself. How crazy would you look if you went outside and allowed your neighbors to see you fighting with your own arm? "Damn you, arm! Every time I go to leave the house, I bump up against that railing. Get your shit together, arm! When we're leaving the house, stop bumping into things. It's painful and distracting!"

Now, how is the fight you just had with your spouse any different? Whatever the issue, it's just as much your issue as your spouse's. Being mad at your spouse is like being mad at your arm. It's just silly. See the truth in that. Notice what you really want. It's rarely about whatever you were fighting about. Instead, pick a different ending to what was started and come back being the person you really are.

"Honey, I just went into the bedroom and saw that you did the laundry… again. I want to apologize for [whatever dumb thing we invariably did during the fight that we now regret]. That basket of laundry reminded me of how much I appreciate you. Let's reset and start again. I want you to know how much I love and appreciate you. I don't like it when we fight. What can I do differently so we can move past this argument?"

Or some variation on that theme. Rather than ignoring what your spouse did for you and the betterment of the marriage, use that act of service to disrupt the fight altogether. I don't know of anyone who, after making up with their spouse, wished they were still pissed off.

Deep Gratitude for What You Already Have

Every moment of every day, we get to choose how we want to be together. If you're not having fun, then guess who gets to change the situation? Interrupting your own pattern and making a new choice is completely up to you. Being happy is a choice. So is being angry and frustrated.

I can hear the other side. "Yeah, but that's only if they will [be/ say/do/have] what we were fighting about!" And that's the trap. Hear me on this. You cannot change the person you married. Let me say that again, you CANNOT change the person you decided to spend the rest of your life with. What you can do is change yourself, and in the process of making changes in yourself, you can invite your spouse into new ways of being with you that will support your forward momentum together.

As much as you might want to, you don't control the person you married. In truth, even if you could, you wouldn't want to. You married your spouse because of their free will and the person they were when you first met them. The world doesn't need another YOU, so stop trying to turn your spouse into a new person of your own design.

Instead, appreciate what you have.

If you went outside into your back yard and saw a beautiful orange tree, would you do everything in your power to turn that orange tree into an apple tree? It's not even worth the energy because it will never happen. But rather than appreciate the oranges, some people think, "Hmm, if I only had apples, my life would be so much better." So they cut down the orange tree and plant an apple tree. And, after taking great care to cultivate an apple tree, they start missing the orange tree they once had. Or they think, "Hmm, maybe having a pear tree will solve all my problems." And the cycle continues.

The illusion is a perfect tree that caters to your every need. Shel Silverstein wrote a book about this called *The Giving Tree*, and it's quite possibly the worst book I've ever read. It's about a tree that gives and gives and gives to a selfish person until there's nothing left but a stump. Which is probably why I laughed my ass off when I recently discovered *The Taking Tree: A Selfish Parody* by Shrill Travesty. I definitely would classify myself as a giver (and not a taker), and these books show what happens in the extreme of both. Givers can be taken advantage of when they allow it and takers can find that there's a point where asking for more has consequences and negative repercussions.

Gratitude is the answer to all of this. When we are grateful for what we have, we can reduce our "wants" and get out of a scarcity mindset (which means living with the false belief that you have very little). Instead, we appreciate the abundance we have in our lives, and that includes the love of our spouse. The minute we can authentically appreciate all the little things our spouse does for us in our relationship, it becomes second nature to take the extra step and verbalize what we are experiencing so our spouse knows, definitively, how much we appreciate them.

THIRD RULE:
WHATEVER ELSE YOU DO,
NEVER END YOUR DAY THIS WAY

"The third rule," said Mr. Knies, quoting Phyllis Diller, "is never go to bed angry," and then he laughed and added jokingly, "stay up and fight."

"Why's that?" I asked him.

"Because you don't want to start the next day with the same issue unresolved."

Seeing the look on my face, Mr. Knies continued, "Look, if you know you're not allowed to keep score and that you can't go to bed angry, it makes you deal with whatever came up that day on the same day it happened. As you get closer to bedtime, you get to decide if the issue is worth staying up late in order to work it out or if it's not that important, and you can let it go."

Damn. That was a mic drop moment for me. So simple, yet so profound.

How do most couple fight? They keep score, stack their arguments, hold grudges and allow small disagreements to grow and fester into huge blow-ups. When couples first fall in love, the other person can do *NOTHING* wrong. Show up late for a date? No problem, I'm just glad you're safe. Forgot something at home? No problem, we'll swing by to get it.

When you first fall in love, you're willing to look past anything and everything that could get in the way of your true love. That euphoric feeling overpowers logic and even the whispering comments from friends who wish to protect you. You'll hear none of it because this feeling of being in love is so powerful, all you want is to keep it going and keep those feelings alive.

Eventually, this euphoric feeling of falling in love begins to fade. And that lack of punctuality and forgetfulness isn't so cute anymore. At that point, are you willing to talk it out when it's happening? Knowing Rule #1 (Don't Keep Score), you're not allowed to bring up every time this thing happens. Without the ability to shove the things that bother you into a proverbial closet and with a 24-hour clock that resets each day, you face a powerful choice. Have the conversation about what's bothering you, or decide it's petty and insignificant and something you can let go.

Past, Present and Future

Where do you want to live in your marriage? When you live in the past, you are full of regret. The first rule of not keeping score forces you out of living in the past. Not having the ability to "go back" to "all the times" your partner did [whatever the issue is at the moment] means you're pulled back into the present.

When you live in the future, you are full of anxiety. The third rule of not going to bed angry forces you out of living in the future and kicking the issue into the next day. Not dealing with a small problem today means the problem is likely to grow and grow until it becomes unmanageable. The third rule of marriage prevents this too.

So what you're left with is living in the present. There's some sappy saying that goes something like, "Every moment is a gift, That's why we call it the present." And while this feels like a greeting card "Thinking of You" nugget, there is something powerful about acknowledging each moment as unique unto itself.

With 20 years of game footage to roll back and watch, I can tell you my biggest fights usually happened when I was (1) Hungry, (2) Tired, and/or (3) Horny. When your tummy is grumbling, your eyes are half-mast, or you're feeling the need to get laid, you tend not to be the most articulate in your arguments. I've noticed the same thing (minus the horny bit) in our kids. When they are hungry or tired, they are not the best version of themselves and any little thing can set them off.

When possible, I do my best to go through this checklist for myself (and whenever possible for the person I'm arguing with) to ensure the frustration I'm experiencing isn't my brain crossing over from a different need I can easily take care of. Pre-meal fights, I've noticed, are a lot more vicious than post-meal.

Exhaustion, however, can work the other way. When you're feeling tired, you get to check in with yourself to see if what you're fighting about is really worth it. Knowing your nice soft bed awaits after the resolution of an argument can be a powerful incentive to become more laser focused on the real issue at hand.

Assuming you've both agreed to follow the *Three Rules of Marriage*, this can also be a powerful tool to use to check in during the disagreement. "I'm just as exhausted as you. I'd love nothing more than to go to bed right now. The only reason I'm still talking about this is because I care about you and our marriage, and I'd like to come to resolution tonight so we can start fresh tomorrow."

And start fresh you do. There's nothing more satisfying than coming to a peaceful resolution and clearing anything that has become a wedge in the relationship before going to bed. It brings closure to an argument as you bring closure to your day. There's something powerful about being clear of any disagreement or problematic issue before allowing REM sleep to take out the emotional trash so you can start with a totally clean slate the next morning.

New Moment, New Opportunity to Expand or Contract Your Marriage

I see the third rule of marriage as a microcosm of the choice we have in every moment of every day. Twenty years of marriage can also be seen as over 630 million moments (630,720,000 for my math nerds – 20 years x 365 days x 24 hours x 60 minutes x 60 seconds). We're not going to make the right choice in every moment of every day because we're imperfect beings.

A career-leading batting average that will get you to the top of Major League Baseball's Hall of Fame is 0.366[6]. (At the time of this writing, Ty Cobb holds the record.) That means, for 1,000 opportunities to hit the ball, you can strike out 634 times and still be the best in the world. The point being that you don't have to be perfect in any way, shape, or form to have a blissful marriage. And you don't need to drag all of your past mistakes forward into your present nor your future. Every single moment of every single day is a new moment to expand your marriage or contract it.

In a given 24-hour day, you get 86,400 moments to play with. Even when you subtract 28,800 seconds for sleeping, that leaves you with 57,600 waking seconds of choice. How many of these are filled with gratitude, appreciation and love? How many are full of anger, resentment and frustration? The choice is yours—every moment of every day.

For argument's sake, what if you look back at how you've been in your marriage up until now and don't like what you see. Let's go further and say that if you were being honest, there have been times when you have been a real asshole up to this point. The choice is still yours to decide to be different. Sure, it may take some time before your partner opens up to your new way of being and sees you being authentic in your choice. That's the price you pay for your history. And the more consistently you choose gratitude over anger, appreciation over resentment and love over frustration, your partner can't help but notice and be impacted by this shift.

The third rule of marriage can support you in starting fresh every day. It can also remind you that you don't have to wait until the day is over to make a different choice. With 57,600 waking moments to choose from, you have an abundance of opportunity to choose the ways of being that will expand the love in your marriage. The more frequently you choose gratitude over anger, the easier it will become for you to make gratitude your default choice.

Being Grateful For It All

When life is going well, it's easy to experience gratitude. When you love your house, your job, your community, your financial statements, your friends and everything else in your life, it's damn near easy to make gratitude your default way of being. But that would be a boring life if that were so. Sure, we say that's what we want, but without challenges, life becomes routine and monotonous.

The real challenge is being grateful for the bad and the ugly side of life. For example, the next time you get cut-off while driving in your car, there's an incredible opportunity to see just how committed you are to being grateful. Imagine being in that moment right now. You've been stuck in traffic for at least a good 10 minutes, waiting to exit when at the last minute some smug, overly confident wanker cuts in front of you without a blinker and nearly causes an accident.

Do you feel your anger rising even as you read that paragraph? We've all been there. The natural reaction might be to flip said person the bird, honk, yell, roll down your window and give the one-finger salute, and/or tailgate for the next mile or so. If that happened in the evening, high beams are also an option. And all of this is giving into your feelings of anger in the moment. It's common because it's the easy choice. What's much more challenging (and therefore growth-orientated) is to smile, take a nice deep breath in and find three things to be grateful for in the exact moment.

For example, I could be grateful that no one in my vehicle was injured. I could be grateful I didn't get into an accident. I could imagine that the person who cut me off just found out one of their parents was hospitalized and is racing to be there before surgery. And I could be grateful I don't have such an emergency that would cause me to drive in that way.

Here's the thing, the choice is ours to make. So let's play this out further. Let's say we choose the one-finger salute and a nice long 60 plus-second horn honk to ensure that person who cut us off knows what a wanker they are. After taking these actions, how will you feel? You might think this course of action is letting off steam, but in reality, it's activating your anger and reinforcing the feeling you continue to have long after the incident. You might further fantasize about what you would say if the traffic allowed you to pull up side-by-side a mile or so ahead. Or you might fantasize about their car breaking down or their future actions resulting in an accident. The more you stew on this incident, the angrier you get until you can easily be set off with the slightest feather touch or off-hand comment. If your spouse was in the car when this happened, you may even end up getting in a fight just to release all that pent-up anger.

Now let's go the gratitude route. Let's say you choose gratitude. What happens after you truly concentrate and authentically feel three things you can be grateful for? You end up shifting your focus from being a victim of being cut off to just how good you have it in your life. In that moment, you choose gratitude, and what results is a letting go of any sense of being slighted and any compulsion toward revenge and getting even with the person who slighted you. If your spouse was in the car, you might even take a moment to share your feelings of gratitude. "Phew. I truly hope they get to wherever they are going safely. I'm sure glad we are safe and accident free. By the way, how's your mom doing?"

Being grateful for it all takes work. It requires being present in each moment and not allowing your emotions to drive you. I'm inviting you to practice in your car because road rage is a very real problem, and there are a ton of drivers who lack sensory acuity. (That means they drive like they are the only ones on the road and unaware of the potential accidents they almost cause every day.) What's more, when you can tackle a big one like being cut off, it makes it so much easier to be grateful for the small things in your marriage.

For example, let's say after a long day's work, you come home and find a number of pots and pans soaking in the sink. If you are already conditioned to be upset because you've had a bad day at work, seeing those dishes in the sink can set you off. "Ugh! You ALWAYS DO THIS! All I want to do is come home and put my feet up, and what I find are dirty dishes in the sink. I guess you left them for me to clean up. Don't worry. I know where the brushes, sponges and liquid soap live. I'll get my hands dirty so you don't have to."

Or you have another choice. "Wow, my spouse must have been cooking and ran out of time to clean up. Poor dear. Maybe I can get through these dishes before he or she gets home and provide a nice surprise. I get to be the dish fairy today. I love having a clean house, and I know this act of service will be appreciated."

Instead of a fight, you get to surprise and delight your spouse. How cool is that? If you can be grateful for dirty dishes in the sink – and I mean authentically grateful – it's going to take a lot more than a few household bumps in the road to knock you out of your journey to a blissful marriage.

Health Benefits of NOT Going To Bed Angry

Happy people live longer. In 2011, the National Academy of Sciences journal concluded a study and reported that, "After accounting for factors including depression, physical health and wealth, the researchers found that the happiest people were more than a third less likely to die." The researchers believe there is a "definite connection between happiness and longevity," and this study is one of many that points to this conclusion. Here is a brief excerpt of the findings:

"A study of 3,800 people aged 52 to 79 found that those who rated their happiness the highest were significantly less likely to die in the following five years than those who were least content.

Even after taking into effect the impact of age, disease and lifestyle factors on people's happiness, researchers found that the happiest group had a 35 percent lower risk of death than the least happy.

Although the results do not prove whether happiness actually causes longer life, they back up previous research which links wellbeing and a positive outlook to longer life."[7]

It just makes sense. When you're happy and you know it, you feel lighter, experience less stress and laugh more. My in-laws, Connie and Richard Knies, are currently 86 and 87, respectively. They are two of the happiest people I know. Despite my completing a full 140.6-mile Ironman, I have difficulty keeping up with them. Seriously, when I come over to their house, they love cooking for their friends and family members, and you rarely see either one of them sit down.

When Connie is not chatting you up, she enjoys painting watercolors, gardening, working at a soup kitchen, being an usher at church, and joining her husband on antique car runs where they take a pristine Buick from 1912 down to Hershey Pennsylvania. That's, of course, when they aren't traveling the world and going on cruises.

Similarly, Richard is into sculpting, building and flying model airplanes, working at a soup kitchen, being an usher at church and, until very recently, was the mechanic who would get under that 1912 Buick and change custom-made parts so the car would run better. Sure, he's had both knees replaced and may be slowing down ever so slightly, but Richard has lived a long and glorious life filled with joy and happiness. A big part of that comes from these Three Rules of Marriage both he and his wife adopted some 64 years ago.

Simply put, it's not healthy to go through life being angry all the time. The third rule of marriage ensures that even if you have one hell of a fight, you don't continue the disagreement into the next day. With every day resetting, you let go of whatever threw you off your course toward a blissful marriage and start fresh. You have the power to give yourself a do-over every day. Why would anyone deny himself or herself that opportunity?

How to Let Go of Your Anger

If anger has been part of your life for some time now, it's going to take some effort to break some of the old habits. It would be fantastic if we could just get up one day and stop being angry for good. For most people, letting go of anger is more of a transition than stopping cold turkey.

And, even once you have decided to let go of your anger, there are both constructive and destructive methods that either support you or make things worse as you look to let go. Below is by no means a comprehensive list. Both the constructive and destructive methods are here to support you as you decide where to go with all of this (and what to watch out for).

Constructive Methods:

1. *Mindfulness.* While mindfulness has become a buzzword in business circles, it's very much applicable to letting go of anger. In essence, mindfulness is about being fully present in the moment and noticing what comes up for you. Without judgment, mindfulness is about listening to your thoughts as they come up and noticing which thoughts support you and which ones you're ready to let go of. There are many books and programs currently available to support you in a mindfulness journey.

2. *Meditation.* My personal favorite. Meditation is a daily practice with as many flavors as there are ethnic foods to

eat. There's the mindfulness flavor where you sit quietly with your eyes closed and allow your thoughts to flow by as if you're observing them on top of a bridge overlooking a river. There is guided meditation where a master talks you through an intentional process. There is an intention mediation where you think of three things you are grateful for, three people you wish to share your gratitude with, and three actions you can take to move your life forward in the direction you choose. And the list goes on.

3. *Yoga.* Until recently, I mistakenly thought all yoga was more or less the same with an emphasis on stretching various muscles and assuming specific positions. Boy was I off base. Recently, I discovered Kundalini Yoga, which "is a blend of Bhakti Yoga (the yogic practice of devotion and chanting), Raja Yoga (the practice of mediation/mental and physical control) and Shakti Yoga, (for the expression of power and energy)."[8] Any flavor of yoga will support your journey toward letting go of anger. Kundalini has the added benefit of a spiritual aspect with its roots in Hinduism.

4. *Martial Arts.* As a Sa Bom (4th Degree Black Belt), I can personally attest to the power of martial arts as it pertains to letting go of anger. I practice in the art of Soo Bahk Do, Moo Duk Kwon, which emphasizes the mind, body, spirit connection. Come for the self-defense, stay for the philosophy and long-life. It is here where I learned the art of "Pyeonghwaloun jasingam" or Peaceful Confidence. When you are skilled in any martial art, you learn just how fragile the human body is and how to "win" a fight before the first punch is ever thrown. It's really powerful stuff.

5. *Gym.* Working out my aggressions via gym equipment has

supported my health in multiple ways. I've become stronger, faster, and more flexible all while working out whatever anger or frustration I'm feeling. Going to the gym may be a longer break in the middle of a fight, but I come back refreshed, focused and ready for resolution.

6. *Athletics.* Any individual or team sport supports your letting go of anger. When I was picked on in high school, I loved flinging my body into the air via a pole vault. Tennis was another fantastic way to work out some pent-up anger. My dad and I used to play some intense games of racquetball, which really helped me get over his divorce to my mom. While I'm not great at it, I love me a pickup game of basketball, soccer, or volleyball. And more recently, I've gotten into trampoline dodge ball. You read that right. Talk about working out your aggression.

7. *Adventure.* Sometimes it's as simple as setting your intention. You can choose to have an adventure anytime, anywhere. A trip to Costco is certainly an adventure since they never keep the same stuff in the same place. So can bargain hunting for anything. Recently, I tried my hand at the paperclip game[9] and converted a single paperclip into a kid's bike, a basketball and several pharma pads (post-it note flavor, not the illegal kind) in under three hours. Watch the TEDx talk of Kyle MacDonald who documented his journey of converting a single paperclip and trading it all the way up to a house!

8. *Travel.* I love the Adam Sandler Saturday Night Live clip[10] where he's a brutally honest tour guide and says coming to Italy won't save your marriage. If you're unhappy at home, you'll be just as unhappy in Italy. That said, what travel

will do for you is get you out of your comfort zone. If you are on a mission to shake your anger, book a trip to India. There you will witness some of the worst poverty clashing with the highest degrees of happiness. People who are dirt poor living in shantytowns can teach you powerful lessons in gratitude. It's life changing. Or you can head on over to the tantra festival in Sweden[11]. A friend of mine recently came back a new woman – I hardly recognized her with the bubbly joy and radiant glow about her. The point is, get out of your box and see how other people live. Get inspired and make a shift.

9. *Art.* Express yourself through any art form you choose. When I was bored with my job and didn't know what I wanted to do next, I took up figure drawing. (This was before I got married.) Not only did I get to sharpen my figure drawing skills, I had the pleasure of staring at gorgeous nude models a few hours per week. That also led to smoking weed with my art teacher and fooling around. It's pretty hard to be angry looking at nude models and networking with the other students. I had a blast.

10. *Journaling.* Initially, this wasn't so helpful for me. Then, I discovered a five-minute per day gratitude journal, and that helped me focus my efforts. If you suffer from blank page anxiety, try a gratitude journal. You can get them on Amazon at a reasonable cost. For five minutes a day, you journal and remind yourself why you're so grateful and your life is a whole lot more awesome than you tend to acknowledge.

11. *Counseling.* For hard-core anger issues, nothing beats professional help. Trained therapists can help you sort out the

root of your discontent, where it all started and techniques to support your letting go. If you're also suffering from deep depression, consider seeing a psychiatrist (as opposed to a psychologist). The distinction is that a psychiatrist has a medical degree that allows them to prescribe medication whereas a psychologist can help you with your mental anguish but without drugs. I'm not advocating the need for drugs, but I do know that for some of my relatives, it really supported their recovery.

12. *Coaching.* When I became a Professional Certified Coach (PCC) with the International Coaching Federation (ICF), I began practicing what I preached and engaged not one, but several coaches for different aspects of my life. My business coach supports me as I grow my income. My health coach supports me when I struggle with weight loss or fall off the healthy-eating wagon. My life coach covers all the other bases, and I'm lucky enough to surround myself with several more opportunities for group coaching on top of all that. While no one needs a coach (and that's the truth), everywhere I look the highest performers in the world have at least one and often multiple coaches.

13. *Volunteering.* When you give authentically of yourself with zero expectation of return, something magical happens – the universe conspires to balance the score. I'm serious. It's impossible to be 100% altruistic no matter how hard you try. Each time I volunteer for ANYTHING, I get back more than I give (despite my best efforts to the contrary). Try it. It's freakishly weird. Give a homeless person clothes, toiletries or food, and suddenly someone sends you a gift of clothes or invites you out to dinner. You brush it off as coincidence

until you see the pattern. You send in $100 to your favorite charity and suddenly someone who borrowed money from you unexpectedly pays you back – often for more than what you gave. Don't believe me? Try it out yourself. It's such a freaky game. The more you give, the more you get despite wanting nothing in return. Conversely, if you only give in order to get something back, the majority of the time, that motive ensures utter failure.

14. *Contribution.* Beyond volunteering is any act of contribution. Your selfless acts propel your growth. The more you contribute, the more you grow as a powerful leader. Again, you don't go into contribution for all the growth you receive – it's just a happy, unavoidable benefit. For each position I've volunteered for, I received training and support worth hundreds and thousands of dollars more than the hours I invested in my contribution to whatever cause I'm supporting. Letting go of anger is so easy when you feel so supported. Contribution is this "behind the scenes" option that all the givers in the world have discovered. Givers join hands with more givers and the takers never get invited to the party (and wouldn't come even if they did receive an invitation).

15. *Youth Leadership.* This one is my personal favorite. For the past 13 years, I've been Unitarian Universalist Congregation at Shelter Rock's Senior Seminar Youth Advisor[12] (which is a fancy way to say youth group adult leader). And I'll keep doing this until I'm no longer living in the area. In my first year of service, I became a youth empowerment advocate. Not only are our children our future, they have such powerful fresh thinking. They keep

me young at heart even as my body grows old. Want to let go of any feelings of anger? Watch in awe as high school youth tackle our global problems of social justice, gun violence, hunger and homelessness.

16. *Transformation.* The industry of transformation has exploded in recent years. There are books, audio programs, online courses, and workshops (see below). Sometimes letting go of your anger requires more in-depth work. The industry of transformation can support your desire to get out of your old paradigm and shift into something better. You can also get started via several books that are inexpensive and free when you borrow them from your local library. One of my personal favorites is Eckhart Tolle's *A New Earth*[13].

17. *Workshops.* I have been to every workshop that Tony Robbins offers. I've also completed Part 1, 2 and 3 of Altru Center: A Community for Altruistic Living[14]. Each time I complete a workshop, I break through to another level of awareness, consciousness and beingness. This transformative work feeds my higher self and allows me to see where my ego trips me up. If you're on a journey for self-improvement, there's a lot here to explore and incorporate into your daily life.

18. *Music.* As a teenager, I took solace in listening to my music. The 80s were a fantastic time to work out anger issues through rock and pop. Today, I like to play the piano and lose myself in the sounds I create. Music feeds your soul and has the power to squash feelings of anger. And now it's as easy as saying, "Hey Alexa, play me some classical guitar music." What an incredible age we live in. I marvel at the vastness of available music with a simple voice command in my house. Don't worry, Siri, while you're not as easy to use

as Alexa, you still have value when I'm in my car driving and need support.

19. *Dancing.* My wife loves to bring me to weddings, bar and bat mitzvahs and anywhere music is pumping. Why? Because I don't take myself seriously. I get into the groove and dance like a fool. I can dance to anything, but lately I've enjoyed the line dances my wife likes. There's something about connecting with your fellow dancers and doing structured moves to a familiar song. And, when that's not what the DJ is spinning, I'll take anything with a good beat. *Turn down for what?* Hard to be angry when you're fully present dancing to a song and connecting with those around you. And if you haven't experienced the joy of a silent dance party[15] you owe it to yourself to check it out. Three channels with three separate DJs compete for your attention. All with LED headsets so you can play it anywhere without disturbing your neighbors.

20. *Bucket List.* By now, you should have several ways to shake off that anger. If you focus on the overall theme, you can apply the above list to just about anything on your bucket list. Adrenaline junky? Try parachuting. Just don't die summiting Mt. Everest. You're no good to your spouse if you pick something that endangers your life. Elena jokes that when she starts urging me to get back onto my motorcycle, it means she's done with me, and my services are no longer required. That's because I really miss riding my motorcycle and sometimes talk about getting back on my road bike.

Destructive Methods

1. *Drugs.* By far, the most popular destructive choice to numb

pain and control anger. I began smoking weed when I was only 13 years old. Now that I have teenage children of my own, I can't even comprehend that. The problem with most drugs is that what starts out as a way to "take the edge off" quickly becomes a dependency problem. Self-medication has the unfortunate side effect of not truly knowing how much is enough. Drug addiction leads to all sorts of unwanted outcomes including financial destruction, loss of job, overdose, divorce and a plethora of other negative consequences. The more addictive the drug, the harder it is to let go when you realize you no longer are in control – the drugs have you versus the other way around. Thankfully, the stigma around drug addiction has lessened over the years and rehab options have grown. The medical community is more aware of the problem and non-profits such as Narcotics Anonymous grew in popularity and availability.

2. *Alcohol.* The legal self-medication choice of grownups everywhere. Growing up, neither one of my parents were big drinkers. So it wasn't until college that I was introduced to binge drinking – and boy did I make up for lost time. While I don't consider myself an alcoholic, I choose to never turn my back on alcohol. Every few years, I "dry out" where I choose not to drink for 3 to 12 months. With my Scots Irish background, I have a heavy tolerance and that has led me to some late nights that were not my proudest moments. The problem is that this self-destructive method is often socially acceptable, so it's harder to notice when alcohol has you in its grasp. Luckily, there's an Alcoholics Anonymous (AA) meeting just about everywhere, so if this has been your outlet of choice, try giving up alcohol for 30 days and see if you can. If you can't, better to know now and tap into

resources like AA to help you find better, more constructive ways to let go of anger.

3. *Eating.* Growing up, I was aware of bulimia and anorexia. What I was less aware of was pleasure eating as a means to avoid pain – even though this was right under my nose with my mom's struggle with obesity. Post college, I also turned to food as a means to take some of the pressure off me at work. What's worse, as I became more successful, I had an expense account, which means I would frequently have working lunches and dinners in the best food cities in the world. No surprise. I became overweight and then obese myself. Crash diets didn't help either. What finally worked for me was a combination of transformation workshops such as Tony Robbins and Altru as well as a moderation-based mobile app called Noom[16]. There are so many available resources for support if you find that you have become an emotional eater or you're ready to drop the weight you've put on since college.

4. *Verbal Abuse.* The problem with anger is that if it's just below the surface, it tends to unleash at all the inappropriate times. When releasing the pent-up anger, it's easy to escalate from verbal release to verbal abuse quickly. As the vicious words come out of your mouth, you can't even believe what you're saying in the moment. It feels so good to let go of the anger, you forget that what you're saying is having a direct and lasting impact on the person who is on the receiving end of your lashing out. I've had to write some powerful apology letters to people I've negatively impacted when I was younger, and there are still people in my life I get to have a clearing with. You can never walk back the words that

cut like a knife. The only thing you can do is authentically apologize for being out of integrity with your words and ask for forgiveness. The first person you need to forgive, however, is yourself. Some of the nastiest verbal abuse you've ever uttered was to yourself. Chances are, you've said some shit inside your head that you wouldn't DARE utter out loud to another human being. Begin with a self-apology. When you can release your guilt for how you've treated yourself, it's a hell of a lot easier to apologize to the others you've hurt along the way. Know this was your ego talking, not your higher self. It doesn't excuse the mistakes made, but it does help you distinguish who you really are versus who you were being in the moment.

5. *Physical Abuse.* Nobody wants to admit to physical violence because it's not okay – not ever. When I was young, I was punched and dragged into fights I didn't want to be in. Before my very eyes, the white anger took over, and I saw myself from above, assaulting my attackers with such hatred, I was actually scared I might kill them. This was LONG before I entered into martial arts. I have empathy for loss of control, yet it's always wrong. The only thing to do is to make amends as best as possible and seek help to ensure you don't lose control of your anger—especially physically.

6. *Picking Fights.* This was one I could never understand— especially weaker people deliberately attacking stronger people so they could feel the pain of being punched out. It's self-destructive behavior. At some level, there's a desire to be beat up because the person feels unworthy. Hello darkness, my old friend. When even physical pain feels better than the

numbness, it's time to seek professional help in the form of therapy. *The Fight Club* may have made an excellent movie, but glorifying violence is never the answer.

7. *Road Rage.* Sometimes, driving like an asshole can feel great. It's so much more dangerous than anyone acknowledges and can be a huge problem. Cutting someone off can be miscalculated and cause a serious accident – especially at high speeds. Driving fast enables the rush of exhilaration. But at what cost? Releasing anger this way is a short-term gain and a huge risk of long-term loss.

8. *Binge Watching.* This one is *much* more subtle. When looking for socially acceptable ways of releasing anger and letting off steam, it's Netflix to the rescue. Why deal with what's really going on in your marriage when you can binge watch the latest season of your favorite program. What's more, you can invite your spouse to do it with you and pretend like everything is going well even when your marriage is on the rocks. Don't fool yourself into thinking that everything is okay. If you and your spouse prefer to Netflix and chill rather than engage in a proper sit-down date night where you actually talk to one another, there may be more problems underneath the surface than either one of you realizes. Instead, get off the couch and set-up a proper date night.

9. *Avoidance.* My grandparents on my mother's side were masters as this. Rather than argue and hash out what's wrong in the marriage, the alternative is to go to your separate corners and avoid each other. The good news is that this minimizes the verbal abuse and has the outside appearance of a marriage devoid of problems. But the minute you look

deeper than the surface layer, it's clear the marriage is more of a platonic roommate partnership to defray shared living expenses rather than one built on happiness. Kicking the proverbial can (full of marriage problems) down the road simply delays the inevitable. And, in the case of my grandparents, ultimately allowed for each to remain in their separate corners until the sunset of the marriage when my grandfather passed away, and a few years later my grandmother stopped eating. Neither one of them ever appeared all that happy to me while I was growing up, but there were moments where they both seemed to enjoy each other's company. Looking back, it felt like they remained at a Level 3 Accepting (i.e. "It is what it is") marriage and did very little to overcome the obstacles that appeared to stunt their growth. But what do I know? I was a grandchild who only saw a glimpse of their marriage. What I do know is the avoidance strategy is one based on self-preservation rather than happiness or an effort to have a blissful marriage. It may keep the anger at bay, but it will not lead to a happy marriage.

10. *Do Nothing.* Whereas "avoidance" is about dragging your feet, doing nothing at all is the ultimate in being stuck. For some people, once the marriage plateau has been reached, they persist in the drift. Rather than risking saying or doing something they would regret in dealing with their anger, they simply bottle it up and pretend it doesn't exist. Doing nothing feels stoic, but it's not. Denying problems doesn't make them go away; it just forces the other person in the marriage to make the first move. Too many of my friends stood by and watched as their spouse chose to move on without them. When you see your spouse going hard into

self-improvement with no invitation to bring you along, they are often themselves at a Level 2 marriage point: planning their escape right before your eyes. Denial is a powerful blinder that allows you to blame the other person. Meanwhile, your partner was being totally transparent with you. Despite seeing what they were up to, the choice was to do nothing. "Even choosing to do nothing is still making a choice," says Mark Batterson in his book *In a Pit with a Lion on a Snowy Day: How to Survive and Thrive When Opportunity Roars*. And the consequence is usually separation followed by divorce.

Phew. I have no intention of ending this chapter on such a downer. The point, which we've now expressed in painstaking detail, is Rule #3: Never Go To Bed Angry. Got it? You have many options around how to get rid of your anger. Clearly, holding it in and doing nothing about it is a very poor choice.

When you embrace not going to bed angry, you choose to live in the moment and clear up whatever is getting in the way of your happiness every day. Start your day with gratitude and, ideally, end it the same way. Consider what you accomplished in the day and then celebrate your forward progress. Do that each day, and you will continue to progress and live life on your terms. Not only will this make your marriage better, it will also make you better. As you continue to improve, so will your love for life. That's the way to be.

SHE SAID: ELENA'S VERSION

Hey everyone, this is Elena. Most of these rules of marriage I learned from my parents. They married in 1955 and really have lived happily ever after. They have been my role models in life as well as marriage. My siblings feel the same, but we aren't the only ones. Friends of ours have told us that our parents have been their role models for marriage too. I'd like to share how they have been so successful.

Of course, it helps that both of them are wonderful, patient, kind people. It would be easy to have a great relationship if one angel were to marry another angel, but it's more than that. I asked my dad once why they never seemed to fight.

He said, "I respect your mother so much that even when she says something I disagree with, I have to stop and think about it."

That really struck me. Love and respect causes reflection instead of a gut response, which can potentially be hurtful.

How does a couple sustain love and respect? My parents got some excellent advice when they got married so long ago. The most important of these? Don't. Keep. Score.

Rule #1: Don't Keep Score

This is the most important advice, hands down. Not keeping score means if Bill does something bone-headed, we have a fight, and I forgive him, it is FORGOTTEN. It is IN THE PAST. If, three months later, he does something else that upsets me, that's unrelated, I'm not allowed to bring up the old offense. That's not fair. That's keeping score. Of course, if a pattern emerges and the same issue keeps coming up, then that problem should be addressed. Not keeping score is about not letting the petty things eat away at your romance. One can't have a healthy, happy relationship when each of you has an arsenal of old resentments in your back pocket, ready to hurl at each other when things get heated. Just let it go. If it's forgiven, it's forgotten.

Almost as important is this rule:

Rule #2: It's more important to say I appreciate you than I love you

Sure, it's important to tell your spouse you love them. My parents, however, were told it is more important to let your spouse know they are appreciated. This means thanking them for everything they do for you. Even if they take out the garbage every week because it's their chore, make sure to thank them. If I notice Bill has emptied the dishwasher, I find him and thank him. If he already left for the day, I send him a thank you text. I let him know he is loved AND appreciated.

Rule #3: Ask "How Can I Help?"

This was not one of the pearls of wisdom I heard from my parents, but it might as well have been. I find myself hearing this advice in my head when I'm not doing anything too important, and I see Bill working on something. I may not want to lug things out to the car, for example, but I hear this phrase in my head, "How can I help?" This makes me go ask Bill if I can help him with whatever he's doing. With the both of us working, his chore is done sooner.

More importantly, he appreciates my help, tells me so, and then I feel appreciated and loved. See Rule #2.

Some More Advice...

Mom and Dad have said it's important to set good patterns from the beginning. They were warned that what you do as a couple in the beginning of a relationship, you will continue to do. They knew a couple who bickered a lot when they first met, and decades later, that couple was still bickering.

Mom and Dad were married well before the Sexual Revolution. They were advised by the minister who married them to buy a sex manual and read it together. Good advice for a young couple in 1955. But how does this advice apply today? The minister meant for them to have a frank discussion about their sex life, a significant factor in many happy marriages. Even in today's world, a couple can benefit from better communication by being able to tell their partner honestly what they want and need.

My folks really know their stuff. Bill and I are far from perfect, but we've been really happy together all of this time. I think it's largely because of these guidelines we received from my older and wiser parents. I hope their words of wisdom help enrich your partnership too.

Bill says I'm powerful with a few words of advice, and I'm happy to sum up my thoughts in a few paragraphs. I prefer reading and do not consider myself a writer. However, I agreed to do this—to step out of my comfort zone—because I love Bill, and this book is important to both of us.

Another insight my mom shared with me was to be careful of the habits you form in the beginning of the marriage. Important decisions about chores, such as who takes out the trash, does the laundry, and pays the bills, should be discussed and decided on together. Once a habit forms early in a relationship, it can quickly become an expectation without being deliberate about it. This can lead to avoidable tensions in a relationship. That's why communication is so important in the relationship. By talking about the things that need to be done, both partners can agree on what each prefers to do and what they are willing to do for the good of the relationship even if they don't enjoy a particular chore.

For example, Bill hates making the bed. While I don't love that chore, I prefer a made bed. A made bed makes the room look neat and complete. It's also much easier to make a bed with two people. When I ask for Bill's help, he does it. It just isn't important to him, so he doesn't prioritize it. I tend to make the bed a lot more than Bill does because the act of making the bed really doesn't bother me, and I like the way it makes the whole room look. What I like is that Bill appreciates all the times I make the bed and doesn't miss an opportunity to tell me so. I know he doesn't like doing it, and he sincerely appreciates my efforts when I do it without him.

What I don't enjoy is doing the dishes. This is where Bill really steps up in our relationship because he's on top of them—especially the pots and pans that take a good deal of scrubbing. He takes the lead on keeping the kitchen neat and tidy, and I make sure he knows how much I appreciate him when he does the dishes (see Rule #2). It keeps our relationship positive as we both appreciate that the other is willing to do more of the work in the area one of us doesn't enjoy.

I regularly listen to about 20 podcasts. Bill thought it would be helpful to talk about one in particular, *Savage Lovecast*, because human sexuality is interesting. Sexuality and relationships are interesting.

Advice columns in general are fun, and sometimes I feel like I'm better off than some people. When I think back to my parents being told by their minister to buy a sex manual and read it together, I think about *Savage Lovecast* as a modern-day sex manual. I can see the value of listening to a sex-based podcast and then sharing with Bill about some of the stories and insights I get from it.

It makes me realize how sweet Bill is and how lucky I am to be in a good relationship. It reminds me to be grateful for Bill because there are so many messed up relationships out there.

I'm grateful for many things in my relationship with Bill. We communicate well. We have similar values on a lot of things. We have learned how to fight fair. We are similar and different in just the right amount. We are both grateful for what we have.

One of the reasons I agreed to write this chapter of the book is because so many great couples get divorced. When thinking about why that is, it's a huge question. There's no way to know what's going on in someone else's marriage. I can only talk about ours. That said, one thing I've noticed is that most people wear masks—some wear them better than others. A great couple, or even a great person, may not be exactly as they appear.

Take a narcissist for example. He or she appears quite charming, but at the core, when you get to know that person, he or she is self-centered and tends not to let everyone get extremely close. So many people don't see beyond the facade. But wearing masks is exhausting and can't be sustained in a long-term relationship.

I suspect that at least one reason people get divorced is that eventually the masks are removed, and both people must make a choice to love their partner, warts and all, or exit out of a more complex relationship than they thought they were getting into.

When the moment of truth comes, we are either willing to adjust to each other's unfiltered truth or seek a more basic and surface level relationship.

In some ways, luck plays a part in all of this. I am lucky to have such great role models as parents. I am lucky to be the beneficiary of such great advice from my parents before getting married. And I'm lucky that I found Bill, who is so naturally compatible with me.

My dad likes to say, "I'd rather be lucky than smart." Often "lucky" works out for people more often than smarts do. Although he was referring to things like investments, luck plays more of a role than how smart you are in many areas.

Disagreements and Fighting Fair

Every marriage has its ups and downs. There is no such thing as a perfect marriage. I know my life is better with Bill in it. When we don't see eye to eye, it's important to focus on the issue at hand and not try to win an argument through personal attacks. Keep the disagreement about opposing points of view and determine the best way forward. Fighting fair is about keeping the focus on the issue at hand and doing your best to stay open, for the good of the marriage, rather than rigid and obsessed with winning the argument.

A recent example of this is our current house. In 2005, we moved into a house we both thought was temporary, and we've been in the same home for 15 years now. For the last year, I've been house hunting and not finding what I wanted. We would love to buy another home in the area that we could actually love. The problem is, we can't find anything in our price range we like. I wanted to buy a certain house because I found one I quite liked. But Bill didn't think it was the right financial decision for us.

At first, I was a bit frustrated with him. I had done all of this research and finally found a home I loved. Sure, it was a little out of our price range, but if we really stretched ourselves, we could pull it off. Bill disagreed.

In order to talk it out, we went on a walk together. During the walk, Bill listened to my rationale about how important it is to actually love your home and how I've never felt settled in the house we're in. He asked questions, but didn't interrupt me or hijack the conversation.

Afterwards, he shared his alternative perspective with me. He agreed that we could afford the house if we really stretched ourselves financially. The reason he didn't want to do this was because the house I loved would set us back on our retirement plans. As we talked it out, I had to agree with Bill's arguments.

And that's the thing. We both really respected each other's point of view. We both deeply wanted to see what the other person saw.

It didn't get personal with us. We could talk about things without getting nasty. We wanted two different things, but once I understood his point of view I could align with him.

That's really an important point. Couples must learn how to fight fair. Specifically, attack the problem, not the person. You're not supposed to say, "You always or you never." It's rarely true, and those words put someone on the defensive. By attacking the problem, a couple can work through and resolve just about any issue. When the fight is about each other, nothing good can come from it.

While this book is called *The Three Rules of Marriage*, there are only two critical rules: (1) It's more important to say, "I appreciate you" than "I love you," and (2) Don't keep score. That's all there is. Those are the ones that truly matter. If more couples would follow these two rules, then I believe there would be fewer couples getting divorced and more happy marriages out there.

BONUS #1:
TRANSFORMATIONAL WORK ON LOVE

There are many transformational experts alive today and the one who is my absolute favorite is none other than Tony Robbins. I had the distinct privilege to meet and interview both Tony Robbins and Joe Berlinger for their Netflix special, *Tony Robbins: I'm Not Your Guru*. You're welcome to watch the complete video interview on my YouTube Channel[18].

If you haven't already attended Tony Robbins' *Unleash the Power Within* event, you owe it to yourself to experience this magic while it's still available live. And when you're ready for a complete transformation, treat yourself to his absolute favorite event, *Date With Destiny*.

In each of his relationship segments, Tony Robbins asks two incredibly powerful questions: (1) Which parent's love did you crave the most? And (2) Who did you have to be in order to receive that love?

At the core of these questions is the formation of your blueprint on love. As a toddler, you began to make up a story that parental love had conditions—even though that's not true. Do one thing and you receive love. Do something else and you are ignored. This early life conditioning became our blueprint for who we needed to be in order to receive love from the parent we craved the most.

Through the exploration of our own love blueprint, we get to bring to light all the conditions we have made for ourselves to experience and truly feel love. Ultimately, we discover we've made it brutal to feel positive emotions such as love on a regular basis and effortless to feel negative emotions such as failure. In Tony Robbins language, these are our "Towards Values & Rules" and our "Away Values & Rules." Now I could certainly share my values and rules with you, but that wouldn't make a lick of difference because they are, by definition, my values and my rules – not yours.

The point of this added bonus is to point out that despite our best efforts, we have been conditioned through our life conditions on how we feel and experience emotions such as love, happiness, passion and even gratitude. In short, we developed a blueprint for our life at an early age and never even questioned the rules we gave ourselves.

Now imagine you bought a brand-new computer and then installed an operating system from 1995 (i.e. Windows 95). This old and outdated operating system would make your computer slow and clunky despite the amount of lightning fast hardware you purchased. You'd never stand for this. You'd demand the most up to date operating system in order to unlock the full potential of your computer.

Nevertheless, we carry around the blueprint from our early childhood development and never think twice about it. No wonder we struggle to find the love we so desperately crave. Is it any coincidence the partner we end up with has so many of the love attributes we valued from a very young age? When you watch the Netflix special, *Tony Robbins: I'm Not Your Guru*, you vicariously experience the breakthroughs from the participants in the audience.

What you do *not* experience is the full update of your own operating system. To this day, I have my original *Date With Destiny* poster I created myself over the course of this six-day journey. Hear me when I say this. I don't work for Tony Robbins, and I don't make a dime if you choose to attend this seminar or not. If anything, I've paid my own expenses to volunteer there several times since my experience simply to support the participants with their journey and breakthroughs. (I'm one of those guys with the bright orange shirts, walking around looking for people in the audience who need support.)

I only share this because I personally witnessed several relationships that were on the rocks get repaired in a single day (i.e. "Relationship Day") during *Date With Destiny*. Is this a "magic bullet?" Absolutely not. What I am conveying is that when two people choose to go deep on their relationships, you could do a whole lot worse than a Tony Robbins event as a platform for lasting change.

For me, I entered *Date With Destiny* with more than 15 years of blissful marriage under my belt. And I discovered a whole new level. I wrote a relationship vision for myself, which I have prominently displayed as part of my poster. And it reads:

> *I will continue to have a passionate, romantic, loving relationship with my best friend and lover and never fail to appreciate how lucky I am or how special she is. I will continue to surprise and delight her so that our relationship always feels fresh and as new as the day we first started dating.*

For my part, I have stayed true to this relationship vision for the past four years and intend to stick with it for the foreseeable future. What I got out of my transformational work on love is an opportunity to go deep—to take a time out from all the day-to-day hustle and bustle in order to reflect on what I have and what I truly want in my marriage.

When I returned home, I had a renewed focus on the importance of our regular "date night" as well as all the ways I can (and do) show Elena how much I love and appreciate her. And the more I put into our relationship, the more I receive − just like any selfless contribution. I'm not doing anything *because* I want something back from her. Far from it. My gifts to my wife are purely my way of paying homage to our incredible union and as a means for me to demonstrate my gratitude beyond words.

BONUS #2:
THE FIVE LOVE LANGUAGES
BY DR. GARY CHAPMAN

I want to thank you for getting this far into the book. As I mentioned in the opening, there are already a number of books available on the topic of love and marriage. The one I believe should be required reading for all couples is Dr. Gary Chapman's *The Five Love Languages.*

Simply put, Dr. Gary Chapman has published the definitive work on the five unique love languages different people have. He even offers a free quiz so you can learn what your love languages are, and if you have your spouse take the quiz, you will also learn what his or her top languages are. Just go to www.5lovelanguages.com in order to take the quiz.

The five love languages include:

1. Receiving Gifts

2. Quality Time

3. Words of Affirmation

4. Acts of Service (devotion)

5. Physical Touch

Where so many marriages get it wrong is that we think individual love languages fuel our partner, and often, that's not the case. I got lucky in that both Elena and I have words of affirmation as our top love language and a blend of quality time and acts of service as our secondary love languages. I skew more acts of service for my secondary love language, and she skews more quality time.

After reading this book (a good 18 years into our already successful marriage), I saw that we actually incorporated four out of the five on a regular basis and all five from time-to-time throughout our history. Receiving gifts was the weakest language for me as I grew up on the lower-end of middle class, and gift giving was reserved for major holidays such as birthdays, Christmas and Easter.

It never even occurred to me to give gifts on a regular basis outside of the holiday season. Once I was out of college and officially on my own, I dreaded buying gifts for all of my family members, so as soon as I had the opportunity, I let go of this love language (at least for the most part).

Sure, on anniversaries I'd throw down. But I was aghast to learn about "push presents." WTF? You mean I'm supposed to give my wife a gift after having a baby? Not something for the baby, but something for her? (Elena never asked me for one, by the way, but I did get pressure from my work colleagues). I questioned if this was yet another marketing move by the diamond industry to hawk more jewelry. Looking back, I see now I was so anti-manipulation prone that I wasn't open to the idea of a gift honoring my wife after birth. So what if she carried a baby inside her belly for nine months and then went through excruciating labor pains – TWICE – just so we could have our two incredible boys. These days, I get satisfaction delivering on some killer anniversary presents.

You'll notice that the Second Rule of Marriage, "It's more important to say I appreciate you, than I love you" roughly follows Love Language #3: Words of Affirmation. The reason I am sharing this bonus section here with you is that if your spouse's primary love language is NOT Words of Affirmation, then do yourself a favor and update your own Second Rule of Marriage to coincide with your spouse's primary love language. That means, buy and read the book, then have your spouse take the quiz. The Second Rule of Marriage can then be modified as follows:

1. It's more important to ensure your spouse **Receives Gifts** on a regular basis than it is to tell your spouse you love him or her.

2. It's more important to carve out sufficient **Quality Time** on a regular basis than it is to tell your spouse you love him or her.

3. Note, if your spouse's primary love language is **Words of Affirmation**, then keep the Second Rule of Marriage the same, "It's more important to say I appreciate you than I love you."

4. It's more important to ensure that your spouse receives **Acts of Service (devotion)** on a regular basis than it is to tell your spouse you love him or her.

5. It's more important to ensure that your spouse receives the right amount of **Physical Touch** on a regular basis than it is to tell your spouse you love him or her.

The other rules would apply directly as written. After reading Dr. Gary Chapman's *The Five Love Languages*, I kind of feel like I dodged a bullet. My father-in-law's advice for the Second Rule of Marriage just so happened to work for him, his wife Connie, me and my wife Elena because for all of us, of our primary love language was **Words of Affirmation.**

In passing on the Three Rules of Marriage, I want to be sure you modify your Second Rule to fit the unique language of love your spouse has so you continue to fill their love tank and not get thrown off by delivering words of affirmation when their primary love language is one of the other four listed above.

Bonus #3:
How Marriage Coaching Is Different Than Marriage Counseling

And finally, since I've been asked this question a number of times, I'd like to provide my unique perspective here on the difference between marriage coaching and marriage counseling. They are both powerful tools when used properly and for the right set of circumstances.

When to Use Marriage Counseling

Just because you see a marriage counselor doesn't mean your marriage is failing. That was the first lesson I learned from my aunt, Jody Leader, who is a successful therapist in the Boston area. In speaking with both her and my uncle, Paul McLean, I discovered that having someone trained in therapy who can support each of your visions for your marriage can be a powerful process in supporting the continued growth in your marriage.

Rather than having the blowout fights, marriage counseling can be used to support the desired outcomes of both spouses. It's about having a professional who is licensed in therapy to support the exploration of what's working, what's not working and what can be added, changed or modified in order for both spouses to achieve their desired results in the marriage – usually happiness and love.

When to use Marriage Coaching

Whereas a trained counselor will offer professional opinions and advice based on research, a certified coach that is part of the International Coaching Federation (ICF) is trained to offer no opinions or advice. Marriage coaching is best leveraged when one or both parties would like to hold space to process what's coming up in the marriage and explore their own answers to profound questions that lead to self-discovery and powerful breakthroughs.

A marriage coach will support you in exploring the best answers for your own life and relationship. Moreover, the marriage coach won't take the bait when you ask them for a solution to the problem you face. Why is that? Because they refuse to rob you of the self-discovery process. While therapists may follow a similar path of self-discovery, they often are more structured and based in the medical field. That is to say, marriage counselors are psychiatrists[20] and psychologists who have specialized education, training and experience helping people.

Which is Better?

Ah, that's a trick question. That's like asking what's better, an apple or an orange? A Philips head screwdriver or a flathead screwdriver? Coaching and counseling are both powerful tools to support your marriage growth. Some couples choose to have both in their lives as they both serve different purposes. Some prefer the mental health aspects of counseling. Others prefer the non-advice structure that comes as part of the coaching modality.

The only "wrong" way is to know definitively there's a problem in your marriage and choosing to take no action. That's a poor choice no matter how you slice it.

So What's Better, Together or Solo?

Another personal choice. The advantage of couples counseling or coaching together is that you both can share what you're going through in front of each other while in a safe space. When you and your spouse are willing to be vulnerable, change can happen in an instant. You don't need either a counselor or coach for that to happen. It helps when you have access to a professional who ensures you both can process what you're going through in a safe space. It avoids the personal attacks and allows for more direct processing of what's coming up for you and your spouse.

When receiving solo counseling or coaching, you get to put it all out there without interruption or your spouse's interpretation. This can be especially helpful when you realize the person who needs to change is you. Not everyone is that clear coming into the support he or she needs. Specifically, the deep understanding that you CANNOT change your partner – you only have the power to change yourself. If you're already clear on that point, solo support can ensure you move quickly to remove any blocks you may have from creating the change you want to see in your marriage.

Stop Talking About It and Take Bold Action Now

Ultimately, the only way you'll know if either coaching or counseling will work for you is to book an appointment and give it a shot. For health insurance that includes counseling as a covered benefit, a list of available counselors can be attained directly from your health insurance. Marriage counselors typically see you (and/or your spouse) in person. For more details on selecting a marriage counselor that is right for you, check out "How to Choose a Marriage Counselor."[21]

THE TRUTH IS...

Now that you've heard both sides of the story, it's time for some universal truths. Here's the challenge with that – these truths have been experienced and have come to be understood via observation. Let me illustrate that point by a story my father told me when I was a little boy.

The Principal and the Ball

Once upon a time, a principal wanted to teach her students a powerful lesson in perspective. Rather than just explaining what she wanted to share, she decided to have each student in the school have an experience and then share that experience. There were about 350 students in the school, and so she gave each of the children a blindfold and had them put it on. Once the blindfold was secure, she had each of them hold hands, and she walked them into a large gymnasium.

As they entered the room, she had the children make a large circle facing in so they were all facing each other. When the principal was satisfied that all the students were standing in the right spot, she instructed each of them to stay in the exact spot where they stood and silently remove their blindfold. Once that was done, she asked them to take a moment to observe what they saw in front of them.

After a minute of allowing all her students to absorb what they saw, she then called on a student who was standing in the center of the west side of the wall to describe what she saw.

The student answered, "It's just a basketball painted **blue** suspended from the celling. I don't get it."

With that, a student on the opposite (eastern most) side of the gym said, "Well, you must be color blind, because what's actually suspended from the wall is a **red** basketball."

At that point, multiple voices started talking at once, and no one could hear each other. So the principle asked all the children to be quiet so she could call on individuals and all could hear what they were saying.

She picked someone standing in between both children at the northern most point in the gym and asked him to describe what he saw.

"I see what the problem is. The ball is painted *blue* on the right side of the wall, and *red* on the left side of the wall."

To which a student opposite him raised her hand. When she was called on, she replied, "Actually, you're close, but don't have it just right. The ball has two colors, and they are split 50/50, yes. But it's *blue* on the left and *red* on the right."

The principal allowed the children to go around and call out what they saw and each one saw something different. No one saw it exactly the same.

"If I had to estimate, I think the percentage is 10% **red** and 90% **blue**." To which the person standing directly across would see the opposite – 90% red and 10% **blue.**

Eventually, the one student stopped looking at what she saw and really started paying attention to what she was hearing and put it all together. But by that time, no one would listen to her – let alone believe her. Each student felt that what he or she saw was the truth. And, more to the point, the *only* truth.

After a while, the principal asked everyone to remain silent and allowed the students to walk wherever they wanted to in the gym. Each student could see the ball from any angle he or she chose. Given the freedom to walk around, it was much easier to observe the basketball from all angles and see clearly that it was painted half red and the other half blue. When standing in the exact same spot, however, the distance and angle showed a very different picture depending on where that person stood in the gym.

Are You Standing In One Spot?

When it comes to your marriage, are you stuck in one spot, seeing one point of view and determined to be right? Is your experience of your marriage *your* truth, or *the* truth? How willing are you to see your marriage from your spouse's perspective? How willing are you to invite in new and outside points of view so you have all the information? Do you dismiss any feedback that doesn't neatly fit into your established perspective, or are you willing to seek out new perspectives so you can see the bigger picture?

To anyone who is free to move around the gymnasium, the truth of the suspected object seems so obvious. But to those who have dug in and are glued to their spot, they would rather be right than know the whole truth. Are you open to new perspectives or are you more determined to be right? It's not a rhetorical question. Some people are willing to listen to and seek out all the available information. Others gather what information they perceive they need and make a judgment.

This is where the Internet FUCKS US UP on a regular basis. Think about it. When you do a Google search, are you searching for the truth? Or are you searching for evidence that supports your already made up mind? Be honest. The algorithms of today evolve based on successful search results (based on clicks and backed by billions of dollars of ad revenue). The algorithms evolve to show us what we want to see – which often isn't so much the truth as opinions we hold up as facts.

To go deeper here would be to skew the focus of this book, but if you want more on this topic, I highly recommend Mark Manson's bestselling book, *Everything is Fucked: A Book About Hope. T*here he goes deep into how hope has really messed with our progress as a species and how artificial intelligence is likely to take over and correct course for humanity. It's both scary and evidence based.

Seek Out the Experts and Then Decide For Yourself

The point I'm making for this book is that if you really want to experience *the* truth, seek out as many experts as you have access to and be sure to understand where they are coming from. When it comes to working out, you wouldn't want to solicit insights from an obese trainer who doesn't practice what they preach. Nor do you want to listen to marriage insights from someone who has never married or has had multiple divorces. While you can learn from all of these people, it's more important to seek out experts who have experienced (and maintained) the success you desire.

What follows are powerful insights that have been both shared and directly experienced. When Isaac Newton discovered gravity, it was just a hypothesis until it was tested repeatedly and eventually became a scientific law (i.e. the law of universal gravitation). The truths that follow can easily be verified by multiple subject matter experts, and some of them are listed as part of the sharing.

Ultimately, it's up to you to decide for yourself. As I mentioned in the very first part of the book:

> *And that, my friends, is what this book is about. Sure, you can spend the next two decades fumbling around trying to figure out love and how to create a blissful marriage, or you can go straight to the source. That's NOT me (or Elena) by the way, it's actually YOU. You are the source of the most epic and blissful relationships of your life – including marriage. What I found, however, is that having some foundational rules really helps direct your focus, language and therefore your outcome.*

So in addition to the Three Rules of Marriage, the truth is:

1. Marriage Is Different Than Falling In Love

2. You'll Spend More Time Doing Errands Than Having Sex

3. You Are Responsible for Your Own Happiness

4. Filling Your Spouse's "Love Tank" Will Change Everything

5. When You BOTH Feel That "I'm the Lucky One," Then You Both Are

6. There Is a Formula for Happiness

Marriage Is Different Than Falling In Love

You may not remember all the things you learned in school growing up, but you most certainly remember your first kiss. Think back to all the nervousness, the excitement and the electric spark sensation when it finally happened. You can easily remember the experience of all the people you fell head over heels in love with – starting in early childhood education to the present. The problem is when people confuse the falling in love experience with what marriage is really about.

I was a late bloomer. When I met Lisa, we were a bunch of kids doing door-to-door selling for my local newspaper, *The Press Democrat* (in Santa Rosa, California). I was excellent at driving subscription sales because I authentically enjoyed connecting with people and discovering why they didn't already have a newspaper subscription. I was playful, funny, and I interrupted people's patterns. They wanted to shoo me away, but once they smiled or laughed, they stayed for the entertainment value (and usually signed up with me).

Lisa, like all early teenage girls, was much more mature than I was. She seemed to have boys around her all the time, so I observed but stayed hidden in the background.

One day, she got tired of waiting for me to ask her out, and she confronted me. "What's the deal with you? I see you looking at me, but you never seem to want to talk. Is there a reason you haven't asked me out?"

I was a deer in the headlights. This girl was SO far out of my league. I couldn't imagine why she would spend two minutes with me, let alone ask me why I wasn't interested in her. When I recovered, I immediately set the record straight. "I think you're the most amazing girl I've ever seen. I didn't want to be rude because it looks like you already have a boyfriend. I didn't approach you or ask you out because I assumed you were already with Tony."

"That guy? Please. He thinks he owns me and doesn't know the first thing about me or what I want."

In my head, I was ecstatic. Was this my lucky day? How could Lisa be interested in ME? But I'd have time to digest all of this later. The time was now and this was my moment. I needed to think quickly and act.

"Do you like the fairgrounds?" I asked.

"Sure. Why?"

"Would you like to go with me to the fairgrounds this Saturday?"

"You mean, like a date?"

"Yeah."

"Okay. Let me give you my number."

And just like that, I was in. Lisa approached me to see what the hell was wrong with me, and in response, I set up my first date. Thankfully, the day at work was wrapping up, so I didn't have to play it cool for too long. When I got dropped off, I was so excited

I called my best friend, James, and even told my younger brother, Brian, all about it.

Since neither one of us wanted the other to see our parents, we arranged to meet up at the fairgrounds right after dinner. Fortunately, I had saved up all my money from door-to-door sales, so I could treat without asking for any money from my parents. I bought our wristbands, and then we proceeded to walk around the fairgrounds, going on all the rides while I worked up the courage to kiss her.

When I finally did, it was so incredibly awkward. I took her behind some building where we were out of view from all the people and went in for the kiss. Lisa, not new to any of this, was happy to oblige. After the first kiss, I confided that I was so nervous.

"Why?" she asked me.

"Because you're so beautiful, and I'm just me."

She smiled and let me hold her hand for the rest of the night.

The best part for me, however, was when the coolest kid in my seventh-grade class, John Peterson, saw me. His jaw dropped, his expression making my night. It was external validation of what I already knew—Lisa was so far out of my league, yet here I was walking around the fair, holding hands. The feeling was euphoric.

The Chemical Release of Falling In Love

When you listen to song lyrics, falling in love has often been described similar to taking drugs—for good reason. That's what's actually happening inside your brain. At the risk of getting too scientific here, there are three distinct chemicals released when you kiss romantically: dopamine, oxytocin, and serotonin. These three chemicals light up the pleasure center of our brains—the same areas of our brains activated by *heroin and cocaine!*

When you do a Google search on the chemicals released when you kiss, you'll find a great article by the British Council called, What's in a kiss? The science of smooching. The following is an excerpt from that article:

What happens in our brains when we kiss?

The brain goes into overdrive during the all-important kiss. It dedicates a disproportionate amount of space to the sensation of the lips in comparison to much larger body parts. During a kiss, this lip sensitivity causes our brain to create a chemical cocktail that can give us a natural high. This cocktail is made up of three chemicals, all designed to make us feel good and crave more: dopamine, oxytocin, and serotonin. Like any cocktail, this one has an array of side-effects. The combination of these three chemicals work by lighting up the 'pleasure centres' in our brain. The dopamine released during a kiss can stimulate the same area of the brain activated by heroin and cocaine. As a result, we experience feelings of euphoria and addictive behaviour. Oxytocin, otherwise known as the 'love hormone', fosters feelings of affection and attachment. This is the same hormone that is released during childbirth and breastfeeding. Finally, the levels of serotonin present in the brain whilst kissing look a lot like those of someone with Obsessive Compulsive Disorder. No wonder the memory of a good kiss can stay with us for years. [22]

In the same article, researchers found that most people can recall up to 90% of the details of their first kiss, and approximately 90% of cultures around the globe kiss. In other words, this powerful cocktail of chemicals released when we kiss romantically are designed to make us want more – it's part of our sexual drive to procreate and keep humanity alive.

So what happens? Our brain's chemical addiction to kissing leads to falling in love – regardless of whether you have sex or not. Think back to your first true love. Even if you didn't have sex, the feelings of falling in love were there well beforehand. And this is the point where many marriages get off to a rocky start.

How Marriage Is Different Than Falling In Love

Marriage – even a blissful marriage – is *not* about maintaining that euphoric cocktail of dopamine, oxytocin, and serotonin in the pleasure center of your brain. When you fall in love, you experience the extreme pleasure center of your brain light up whenever you are intimate with your lover. Even when your lover enters the room, your heart can skip a beat because you're totally and completely in love.

The mistake is thinking these chemical sensations in your brain can be sustained forever. In sticking with the drug analogy from earlier, that euphoric cocktail of dopamine, oxytocin, and serotonin activates the same pleasure center in your brain as heroin and cocaine. Ask someone who has been addicted to either of these drugs. The only thing you want to do when you're on cocaine is get more cocaine. And the same goes with heroin. The more drugs you take, the more drugs you want and feel you need in order to maintain the high.

Eventually, one of two things happens to the heroin and cocaine users – they wean themselves off, or they hit rock bottom. This is a perfect analogy for those who are chasing the falling in love feeling and keep getting divorced in order to find a new lover who will help maintain that high from falling in love. When I hear someone has been divorced and remarried more than three times, I have a deep desire to talk to them and find out what they attribute to their multiple divorces. What I often hear is "we just lost that loving feeling" or a variation of that sentiment.

Marriage is different than falling in love because it's the partnership, not the dopamine, oxytocin, and serotonin, that keep two people together.

Think about it. What will you do for your partner when you're in love?

ANYTHING! When you're smitten with the chemical cocktail, there is virtually nothing you wouldn't do for your partner. When you're with your partner, you feel euphoric – it's almost an out-of-body experience.

Eventually, however, this feeling fades, and you're left with one of two choices. (1) Build your relationship upon the solid foundation of the love the two of you have created, or (2) Bail out of the relationship and go find someone else that enables you to experience the same sensation of euphoria. In other words, are you chasing the high or are you building a long-term partnership with someone you truly care about?

Sure, during any long-term committed relationship there will be highs and lows – that's perfectly normal. What isn't possible is sustained euphoria. If that's what you're after, attend an Alcoholics Anonymous or Narcotics Anonymous meeting and talk to a community of people in recovery about chasing the high. You never get there. For people in recovery who have hit rock bottom, many gave up everything in a doomed effort to sustain that feeling of euphoria. That includes their money, careers, marriage, children and extended family. Some have robbed, cheated, and stolen whatever they had to in order to maintain the high.

But wait, that's not me! You're comparing chasing that "falling in love" feeling to being addicted to drugs and alcohol.

The two are a lot closer than most would care to admit. When drugs have you, then you are an addict. How is that any different when that "falling in love" feeling controls you? Is chasing that feeling any more logical than chasing the drugs or alcohol highs? This is called sex addiction. Many people (especially women) view sex as love, but they are not the same thing. You can be in love without having sex and you can have sex without being in love. A sex addiction may be more socially acceptable than a drug, alcohol or gambling addiction, but if something (anything) has you, then you're not being your higher self. And that IS the point.

Unpacking the Unexpected Value of Arranged Marriages

In Tim Samuels' book *Future Man: How to Evolve and Thrive In the Age of Trump, Mansplaining, and #Metoo,* he examines the wisdom of arranged marriages:

> *The psychologist Robert Epstein, who has been researching love in arranged marriages, says we should instead maybe look to India, where the motto is: "First comes marriage; then comes love." Love is something to be built over time – and, in the end can actually exceed the happiness of those who married for romantic love.*

> *Indeed, Brian J. Willoughby, from the School of Family Life at Brigham Young University (a Mormon institution not so hot on premarital sex), says this arranged approach can work because it "removes so much of the worry and anxiety around whether 'this is the right person.'" He notes, "Arranged marriages start cold and heat up and boil over time as the couple grow and get to know each other. Non-arranged marriages are expected to start out boiling hot but many come to find that this heat dissipates and we're eventually left with a relationship that's cold."[23]*

When I first heard of arranged marriages, I was repulsed by the idea. How dare anyone take away my freedom of choice? I was already a practicing disciple of the *31 **Flavors** **of Dating*** concept my dad shared with me.

"Son, before you get married, you want to make sure you have dated sufficiently to satisfy all your curiosities so that you are sure in your decision. Imagine walking into a 31 Flavors Ice-Cream store, and the very first ice-cream cone you ever have is pistachio. It's green and delicious. You love it so much, that you vow never to eat any other flavor of ice cream ever again. Your heart belongs to pistachio. Years later, you see how many people love chocolate, strawberry, fudge and all the other 30 flavors you never tried. Now you regret your decision of committing to pistachio before trying the other flavors. You want to date as many people as you can to be sure you want to spend the rest of your life with the person you choose to marry."

This made perfect sense to me, and I was well on my path when I discovered the concept of arranged marriages. That ran totally counter to what my dad had shared with me, so I rejected the idea outright.

That is until I spoke to a few people who were actually in arranged marriages and were happy about it. What I did not know is that the parents who arrange the marriage are incredibly selective. The parents find suitable mates through holistically looking at all the aspects of the marriage – financial, career, values, religion, status, and many other attributes that go well beyond the romantic love and attraction most couples rely on today.

Author Tim Samuels goes on to explain, "Dating itself is a relatively new phenomenon. The idea of going out with someone without any parental interference took off shortly before 1920 in the United States."

We take for granted that freedom of choice is how it's always been, but it's really only been mainstream for about a century here in the US. When you add in mobile apps like Tinder, it's important to take a step back and question the wisdom of where we place our faith in meeting "the one." Given a Tinder app or my parents, I'd trust my parents many times over to have my best interests at heart.

So while I'm not a vocal proponent of arranged marriages, I'm a lot more open to the idea in this age of Tinder, Match.com and dozens of other online services. Algorithms may ultimately win the day. But while we still have free choice, I look to the savvy insights of my elders over a photo-shopped image masking all sorts of views and values I don't align with (and will take several weeks or months of dating to reveal).

The Alternative: Marry Your Best Friend

Sometimes it's plain dumb luck that puts two people's relationship paths together. Before I found Elena, I was a stress bunny. Having kicked off an incredible career at digital marketing pioneer, Modem Media, in 1994, building some of the very first commercial websites, my career had taken off in ways I couldn't even imagine. For the better part of five years, I followed my dad's 31 Flavors of Dating advice.

I dated a woman who was 12 years older than I was and worked in the same company (something we were both afraid anyone would find out about). I would go into New York City and find amazing dance partners who I would end up dating for a while. Whenever I was in a relationship for more than a few months, I would ask myself, "Could this be the one?"

I met Elena in late 1996 in the most bizarre way. I was standing at a Bank of America ATM in downtown Manhasset, New York when I distinctly heard a loud keup (a distinct yell). I stopped what I was doing and poked my head in to what, at the time, was Kwon's Tang Soo Do. Tang Soo Do, which later became Soo Bahk Do for international trademark reasons, is the traditional South Korean military art of karate. It was rare to find a studio of Tang Soo Do as the Taekwondo franchises had blossomed and took over the traditional military style.

This is important because when I signed up to take Tang Soo Do Moo Duk Kwan, it was a continuation of the style I learned in college. There were precious few studios like this one nearby. The next closest one was in New York City, some 40 minutes away by train.

When I first met Elena, she was studying in this studio and was already a red belt (three promotions away from black belt). The moment I saw her, sparks flew for me. She was drop-dead gorgeous, and the fact that she was a martial artist said something to me — that she not only knew how to defend herself, she also stuck with it long enough to rise through seven belt promotions. I, myself, was a red belt, so we were often paired up together. More than that, because of the class schedule, we spent most Friday nights together with the rest of the students. Our karate class began at 8pm and ended at 9:30pm. Most of us didn't want to run home, take showers and spend another 40 minutes going into New York City. Instead, we ordered in pizza and beer and hung out together.

The more I got to know Elena, the more I really liked her. But I never asked her out.

The story I told myself was that if we dated and it didn't work out, one of us would have to leave the studio. As we were both roughly two years away from testing for our black belts, I didn't want to risk it.

Until one day, Elena disclosed that she was moving back to Maryland to be with her college roommate. She was thinking about going back to school, and since her sorority sister was still living there, this would give her some time and space to consider what she wanted to do next in her life.

Perfect! Once she had moved down to Maryland, it was totally safe. I could ask her out, and if things didn't work out, I could still complete my training and get my black belt. The thing was we had developed a very close friendship over the roughly two years we knew each other. Not dating each other meant we could confide in each other about anything and everything. We spent so many Friday evenings together platonically, that there was none of the "mask removal" nonsense when it came to dating each other.

When I asked Elena out, she was shocked. In truth, I didn't so much as ask her as I surprised her with a kiss. We were alone back in her parents' home, talking about something when I went in for the kiss. She was taken aback, but then she responded in kind. Then she needed to collect her thoughts, so I excused myself and left the house. Long story short, we only dated for about three months before I proposed.

Having had the opportunity to truly know Elena ahead of time left no doubt for me. I knew who she was (in some ways probably better than she knew herself). There was none of the gamesmanship I had traditionally experienced with dating. Mask free, we kept being ourselves, only we allowed the romance to catch up to our already close friendship.

By the time I asked Elena to marry me, I was already friends with her sister Nancy, her brother Eric, her brother-in-law Jack, and Nancy and Jack's amazing kids, Drew and Laura. I loved Elena's family like my own and welcomed the opportunity to become part of this incredible family.

After all, I wouldn't be sharing these Three Rules of Marriage with you if I hadn't first gotten to know Elena's parents. Well before I ever asked Elena out on a date, I sat at her Thanksgiving table at least once (and probably more than once) as Richard and Connie have a habit of hosting singles and strays who find themselves away from their own families. I had been an adopted son well before I was their official son-in-law.

Marriage is different than falling in love. Yes, I fell in love with Elena long after we established our bonds of friendship and family connections. I experienced the person I wanted to spend the rest of my life with for a good two years before I asked her to marry me. If Elena grows up to be her own version of Connie Knies some 40 years from now, I couldn't be happier. I truly hope my father was right in that the apple doesn't fall far from the tree.

And, if I can grow up to be half the man Richard Knies is, then I will have lived a life of purpose, contribution and valor. Richard may never have a statue erected of him or a college building named after him, but he gave me these Three Rules of Marriage, and I'm committed to sharing his wisdom with as many people as I possibly can before I am dead and gone. The world will be a better place when more people are in stable marriages that support their growth and contribution in the world. While many men fight their way up the corporate ladder to be best IN the world, Richard has lived a life of contribution. At least in my opinion, he is best FOR the world. And that one word "FOR" makes all the difference.

[Fade to black.]

You'll Spend More Time Doing Errands Than Having Sex

Wait, we're not done? Come on. That's a perfect place to end the book, don't you agree? Oh, that's right. "And there's more!"

This one will be short – I promise. The insight is powerful yet often overlooked. My father-in-law, once said to me, "You know, you'll spend more time doing errands than having sex. So it's important that the two of you like each other and respect each other's opinion."

The context came from a question I had just asked him.

How Is It That I Never See The Two Of You Fight?

"It's not that we don't argue or disagree," he explained. "It's that I respect Connie's opinion. If we disagree about something, then we talk it out. If Connie feels strongly about something, then I listen up. She knows me and understands what's important to both of us. Now, that works both ways. If, after she explains her perspective, I still don't agree, then she does the same for me. She listens. And, at the end of it, we usually both learn something and decide how best to proceed. You know, you'll spend more time doing errands, than having sex. So it's important that the two of you like each other and respect each other's opinion."

Mic drop.

Richard has that effect on me. He's a quiet man by nature, but when he speaks, I not only listen, I do my best to take notes. His Three Rules of Marriage supported me many times throughout my 20 years of marriage to his daughter. When he chooses to drop another pearl of wisdom on me, I listen—DEEPLY. And then I act on his insights.

Sex Is Incredibly Important In the Marriage

Over the 20 years that Elena and I have been together, our sex life has gotten better each year. I know that may sound off to you, but it's the truth. Early in our marriage, Elena suffered from vulvodynia[24], so sex was a lot harder than it should have been. Imagine every time you had sex, you experienced burning, stinging, irritation, and rawness that was *not* caused by an infection, skin disorder, or other medical condition. That's vicious.

After the birth of our second child, it went away. But even after the pain left, the psychological trauma stuck around. If every time you had sex it hurt (and you've been having sex for several years despite the pain), it takes a while to disassociate from the pain even after it's truly gone.

With the benefit of time and absence of pain, our sex life blossomed, and it truly enhanced our marriage. Still, what Richard said is absolutely true. We still spend the vast majority of our time together in the kitchen preparing meals and cleaning dishes or in the living room sorting laundry. I can't imagine a life where I loved the sex but couldn't tolerate my partner outside of that. Or the opposite where I loved my partner and enjoyed spending time together, but the sex was rare to never. For most, a blissful marriage requires both, even if more of the time is spent doing the mundane tasks to keep the household going.

Finding Joy in the Monotonous Chores and Simple Pleasures

How does one find joy in the monotonous? The first step is realizing it's a choice to feel how you want to feel in any given moment. Let's take washing dishes. Spoiled as a child, I never had to wash any dishes. My mom claims she loves washing dishes – it's her Zen – so she never minded doing them, and none of the boys in the household minded letting her.

So you can imagine the shock in college and then post-college when the Dish Fairy disappeared, and the same dirty dish I left in the kitchen sink waited as long as it needed to until I cleaned it myself. What's worse, as I did those dishes, I grumbled under my breath every minute about how unfair life was. "Stupid dishes, why do I have to do them? I mean, isn't my time more valuable than this? I just launched websites for MasterCard, CBS and AT&T. I bet those executives don't wash their own dishes." And all the rest of the nonsense.

One day, I saw it completely differently. "Wow, how cool is it that I'm married and have a wife that I love dearly? I know she would appreciate it if she came home to a clean house, so I'm going to make sure I do my best never to leave a mess for her to clean up. In fact, whenever I see one of her dishes, I'm going to jump in there and do it for her before she even as a chance to think about it." (Elena would like me to point out that she does the dishes too.)

What changed was my attitude. Washing the dirty pots and pans was exactly the same chore I'd been doing (albeit begrudgingly) since college. One day, I just decided to see what I was doing as an act of service instead of as a chore. I envisioned myself making an offering to my wife goddess Elena the same way the ancient Romans would make an offering to their gods. And, because of Rule #2 ("It's more important to say I appreciate you than I love you"), guess who often got recognized for my acts of service? "Oh, honey, you didn't have to do my dishes!"

"I love and I appreciate you. Why wouldn't I do those dishes?"

"Wow, I don't know what I did in a past life, but I seriously don't deserve you."

"You say that, but we both know that I'm the lucky one."

"Boy, do I have you fooled. Not only am I the lucky one, you think you are. Seriously, I don't deserve you."

And how good do both partners feel with an exchange like that? Even if Elena doesn't tell me how much she appreciates me, she makes enough deposits in my emotional bank account that I know it to be true. I'm filled up with love because she tells me how much she appreciates me, and I, overflowing with feelings of love, put it right back on her. And so it goes.

Honestly, my view of house chores has completely changed over the 20 years we've been married. I see them as a way to keep a tidy house, abundant with food, drinks and clean clothes. My wife is a total neat-freak when it comes to how clean the house is. Everything has its place, and I've come to value how organized she is and, therefore, how organized our household has become.

Chores Are Neutral

Simply put, all chores are neutral – they are neither positive nor negative. That is until we put our emotions on them. For years, the last chore I have weaseled out of whenever I get the chance is making the bed. Sure, if I know company is coming over, I'm happy to make the bed presentable, but otherwise, I don't feel a compulsion to make it every morning. Besides, I'm usually the first one out and the last one in, so it's rare that I find myself with an empty bed that needs making.

Tucking in blankets is no big deal. It just is. Elena prefers to have a made bed, and I admit that when I'm ready to go to bed, a made bed is more appealing. The act of making the bed is, in fact, neutral. When I resist making the bed, it's because I interpret the chore as negative, and I do my best to avoid the negative in my life. When I look at my resistance to making the bed (I can hear Tony Robbins in the back of my head saying, "What resists, persists"), my resistance is silly. I'm making a neutral chore feel negative in the same way I make washing dishes feel positive.

Both choices are available to me. The chore is neutral. How I feel about doing the chore is the emotion I put into the chore and therefore my experience of doing the chore. When I wish to stop resisting a chore, I simply need to reframe my attitude about it and recognize it for what it is—a neutral thing I get to decide how I feel about.

Since I'll spend more time doing chores with Elena than having sex with her, it's a fantastic idea to keep all chores neutral or positive so my experience of them fills me up rather than bums me out and deflates me. Besides, I've since learned that men doing household chores can be a big turn on. When we're by ourselves, who knows? Perhaps the time we spend doing the errands will lead to sex. It certainly has before. ;-)

YOU ARE RESPONSIBLE FOR YOUR OWN HAPPINESS

Duh, right? Well, not so for everyone. One of the things that trips up newlyweds is the mistaken notion that their partner is responsible for their happiness. When you're head over heels in love, that cocktail of dopamine, oxytocin, and serotonin released in the pleasure center in your brain is not only intoxicating – it's addictive.

When these drugs released inside your brain simmer down, it can be a bit of a letdown and leave us wanting more. So while we know logically that we're responsible for our own happiness, the cocktail of dopamine, oxytocin, and serotonin makes us push logic to the side and crave for more of what's being released in the pleasure center of our brains. We then seek that renewal from the very partner who lit the spark that delivered these drugs inside our brain. When your partner is balancing their newfound responsibilities as a spouse, financial provider, homemaker, cook, cleaner and everything else, those romantic experiences can become less frequent than when you were first in your courtship.

So what happens? The blame game begins. "You never..." and "You always..." show up where they never existed during the initial courtship. The honeymoon is literally over, and what's left in its place are all the bills, thank-you notes, and a plethora of stuff that, while you may have registered for it, you don't exactly know where to put it. Juggling all of these responsibilities can be daunting. The last thing you need piled on top is a spouse who is unhappy and looking for you to "fix it."

Effective Communication Is Critical

Nick Morgan, my public speaking coach, used to tell me, "Effective communication is NOT what I as the speaker say, it's what you as my audience hears."

While this golden nugget was shared as part of an audience-centered public speaking training, it's applicable right here.

When married couples talk past each other, the lack of effective communication begins to bring all sorts of unwanted negative feelings into the space of the marriage. Taking responsibility for your own happiness means effectively communicating with your spouse – especially when the conversations are more difficult in nature.

Your own pursuit of happiness can sometimes conflict with your spouse's pursuit. When in a marriage, the ability to effectively talk out your vision for the future helps you work through conflicting views and any inhibitors that stand in the way of future growth.

While the hard conversations may be uncomfortable, not having them is even worse. Better to know where your spouse stands ahead of time than making bad assumptions that lead to heavy conflicts.

Know When to Compromise

Before I met Elena, I rode a motorcycle and completed a static-line parachute jump. Even after we were married, I still rode my motorcycle, and just for fun, I began working toward my recreational pilot's license. Then my first son, Will, came into our lives, and Elena wanted to be sure that I stuck around for a while. As much as I didn't want to, I agreed to stop the pursuit of my pilot's license (even though I was one check ride away from my solo), agreed not to sky dive and gave up my motorcycle.

Adding more safety and precaution to my adult life was certainly the right thing to do, but that didn't mean I was excited about it. There's nothing quite like the rush of a motorcycle, the thrill of being in control of an airplane or the adrenalin rush of jumping out of one. But we talked it out, and I saw that while these thrill adventures had a relatively low probability of death (given all the precautions I took), the burden of having Elena raise our kids without her husband and their father was too much of a preventable risk. So I redirected my passions for adventure toward international travel, martial arts, and scuba diving. I was willing to make the compromise for the good of both our marriage and the raising of our family.

What I would not compromise on was my values or the big picture of our life together.. I was willing to give up some of the dangerous things I enjoyed,, but not my vision for our family unit. Marriage truly is a give and take. Knowing where you're willing to give is part of taking responsibility for your own happiness. Only you know what your non-negotiables are. Just make sure your spouse is also aware of them and that you're willing to give up on the smaller stuff that isn't as critical to your long-term happiness.

FILLING YOUR SPOUSE'S "LOVE TANK" WILL CHANGE EVERYTHING

Earlier, I referenced Dr. Gary Chapman's book, *The Five Love Languages*. I stand by my sentiment that this book should be required reading for all newlyweds. In his book, Dr. Chapman talks about how important it is to fill up your spouse's love tank.

I equate filling up your spouse's love tank to having a full meal and a good night's rest before making important decisions. Great decisions are not made when you're Hangry (hungry + angry) and exhausted. The same can be said for being in a relationship when your love tank is running on fumes.

When you don't feel loved and appreciated, any little thing can set you off. "Oh sure, go to your poker game with your guy friends AGAIN and leave me here all alone, why don't you. I guess I'll just take care of the kids like always!" (Elena has never said that to me, by the way. I'm just illustrating a point here). That sentiment is a lot less likely to be felt when your spouse just had an epic date night the previous evening and feels totally loved and appreciated. Instead, she's more likely to say, "Be safe tonight and call me if it gets too late and you need a ride home. I want you to stick around." Same event: going to poker night with the guys. Two totally different feelings based on how full or empty my *spouse's love tank is.*

I'm lucky. Really, it was dumb luck. My wife's primary love language is the same as mine and because of Marriage Rule #2 (it's more important to say I appreciate you than I love you), we both filled up each other's love tank from the very beginning of our engagement (let alone our marriage). And because each of our love tanks are topped off every day, we are very understanding and forgiving when one of us screws up.

When Your Spouse's Love Tank Is Full, They Assume Good Intentions

It comes down to this. When your spouse's love tank is full, they assume good intentions about you always (or at least most of the time). If something seems "off," they ask rather than assume the worst. You're given the benefit of the doubt because of how you've shown up consistently in the marriage.

When your spouse's love tank is running on empty, good intentions are not assumed. In fact, it's the opposite. Every event and every comment is analyzed for evidence that you're up to no good.

Having an empty love tank is like working in a restaurant's kitchen when you're starving. Food is all around you, but you're not allowed to eat it. Having an empty love tank in a marriage is the same way. You're expecting to feel loved by your spouse, but you simply do not. Instead, when you have an empty love tank, you just feel trapped, broken down and isolated. When you're feeling this low, how can you possibly want to stay in the relationship?

And Yet, Filling Your Spouse's "Love Tank" Will Change Everything

The brilliance of Dr. Gary Chapman is that he acknowledges

it's rarely ever too late. Even if you've not understood your spouse's primary love language for years into the marriage (and thus they are running on empty), the minute you figure out his or her primary love language, you can turn it all around.

As a reminder, the five love languages are:

1. Receiving Gifts

2. Quality Time

3. Words of Affirmation

4. Acts of Service (devotion)

5. Physical Touch

As mentioned earlier, Dr. Chapman offers a free quiz so that you can learn what your own love languages are. I highly recommend that you and your spouse take the quiz. Just go to www.5lovelanguages. com in order to take the quiz.

In the book, Dr. Chapman says if your spouse doesn't want to take the quiz or read his book, just complete a six-week challenge where you surprise your spouse with a big dose of a single love language to gauge shifts in his or her emotional state. That's your feedback. You'll know which language your spouse uses as primary when you notice a shift in his or her actions and attitudes in response to your activating their primary love language.

I know it sounds almost too good to be true. If you want all the observations and research from Dr. Chapman, I recommend reading the book. From personal experience, it's about not forcing the things you want onto your partner. For example, if you are all about physical touch, and your partner is all about quality time, you're going to wonder why your partner is deflecting your physical affection and mad at you for not spending quality time together. For your partner, being physical may not be "quality" time, and so you're desperately craving more physical connection while your partner can't understand why you don't want to just "be" together, taking a walk or going out to dinner.

Or, put another way, you'll know when your spouse's love tank is being filled up because of how they act when they are around you. Filling your spouse's love tank changes everything in your marriage because when it's full, you both feel the love deeply and consistently. The overall shift in the marriage will be easy to notice as it heads toward when things were at their best.

When You BOTH Feel "I'm the Lucky One," Then You Both Are

When reflecting back on the past 20 years of marriage, I came up with an important distinction I'd like to share. Throughout the entire last two decades, there has been an authentic feeling that "I am the lucky one."

Before Elena, I knew when I dated both above my league and when it became clear that I was settling. When both people agree, then there's a natural shift in the power dynamic. For example, when a beautiful young woman marries an old, but wealthy man who could easily be her father (maybe her grandfather), the power dynamic is clear. She's willing to trade her youth for money and security and he's willing to give away some of his wealth to enjoy the company of a much younger woman.

Moral and ethical judgments aside, you can clearly see the power dynamic. She has the option to use sex to get what she wants, and he'll use his control over money and power to get what he wants. When you remove any feelings of love, the union is based on one of mutual gain and can often work itself out.

But what happens when two people genuinely think they

married up?

This is what happened with Elena and me. If you ask Elena, she'll tell you she's the lucky one because of all of my wonderful qualities ;-)

I, on the other hand, know I'm the lucky one because of who Elena is – especially when she chooses to tap into her innate feminine goddess. Her natural radiant beauty is obvious to anyone who has met her. She's been an incredible belly dancer for nearly two decades in addition to being a powerful, strong woman who can take me to the cleaners intellectually. She cooks, cleans, does multiple errands, and runs a tight ship in our household. She's raised two incredible boys who will turn out to be the kind of men most women think don't exist anymore. She also contributes financial support, does all the heavy lifting around the research for our epic vacations, and somehow makes time to support me when I've had an off day.

You get the picture. The evidence is so highly stacked in her favor it's ridiculous that we even have this conversation. And yet, she genuinely believes that she's the lucky one. I know for a fact that I am the lucky one.

What really matters is that regardless of who is actually right (i.e. "the truth"), our belief that we are lucky as hell to be in this relationship means that neither one of us takes our marriage for granted – not ever.

"I Cheated On You"

A few years ago, I was standing in front of both my sons when I said to my wife, "Honey, I have something terrible I need to own up to. I feel terrible about it. I cheated on you."

Without hesitation, Elena punched me in the arm and said, "You had Ethiopian Food without me?" She was indignant and played the part of a very upset wife. Then all of us laughed about it.

There was never a question that I strayed sexually from our union. "To cheat" was to eat our favorite food without both of us enjoying the meal together. How's that for a blissful marriage?

I do, in fact, count myself lucky to have spent nearly half my life (so far) with a partner who thinks I'm amazing and that she's lucky to be with me. And yes, I feel exactly the same way. Life is too short to settle for a Level 2 ("Planning My Escape") or a Level 3 ("Accepting: It Is What It Is") relationship. We all deserve to be in a Level 5 Blissful Marriage – or at least a Level 4 Happy, Joyful and Desire More Marriage. I'd argue that if you're in a Level 4 right now, it's a beautiful thing because it means you're fully aware of another level to the joy and happiness you're already experiencing.

Even as I enjoy my marital bliss, I know the moment I start coasting and take my marriage for granted, I put it at risk. And I never want to do that. Elena is my rock, and I am the best version of myself because of her. We can debate who the lucky one is all we want – I already know the truth. My evidence that I'm the lucky one is all around me and everywhere I choose to look.

THE FORMULAS FOR HAPPINESS

Ah, the formula for happiness. First, there's not just one formula. I actually discovered and experienced five different formulas, and I'm positive there are many, many more I have yet to discover. So far, here are the most powerful ones I've come across:

1. Tony Robbins' Formula for Happiness, Contribution and the Art of Fulfillment

2. Ray Dalio's Struggle Well

3. Tal Ben-Shahar's Gratitude Formula

4. Tony Hsieh's Purpose & Passion

5. John C. Bogle: Stop Chasing The Rabbit

Tony Robbins' Formula for Happiness

When it comes to a world of transformation, very few people alive today have touched more lives and reached more people than Tony Robbins. I count myself fortunate to have spent one-on-one time with someone who is so deeply dedicated to transforming the lives of millions. So let's kick this off with not one, but three separate happiness formulas I have learned throughout my Tony Robbins journey.

164

The first one is a formula and the inspiration for this section of the book:

$$LC=BP$$

Take a moment to think back to a time when you truly felt happy. What was happening in your life? How old were you? What was going on that made you so happy? When you take the time to unpack a powerful happiness moment, you'll discover that underneath it all, your Life Conditions matched your Blueprint.

You'll find this consistent through all the times in your life when you were most happy. Life conditions are what is happening when you are experiencing joy, happiness and even bliss. Your blueprint is how life is supposed to be – according to you. When your expectations of how life is supposed to be match what you are experiencing in your life, you will be happy.

By the same token, Tony Robbins shared the formula for suffering:

$$LC \neq BP$$

Scary to think that the difference between happiness and suffering can be binary and expressed in a simple hash mark. What Tony Robbins explained is that when your life conditions don't match your blueprint, you experience suffering.

Material possessions don't make you happy. There are plenty of people who can be happy with very little. And this is also why even the richest multi-billionaires can suffer from deep depression and even seriously consider suicide despite all they have accomplished in their lives. When your life conditions don't match your blueprint, you have two options. (1) Change your life conditions, or (2) Change your blueprint.

Changing our life conditions is about removing anything that prevents us from having the life of our dreams. When we clearly see what stands in our way from having what we want, we have the opportunity to remove these obstacles. No one intentionally sabotages himself or herself, but at some point, we all end up doing that. We make decisions that are not the best ones for ensuring we get the outcomes we desire. Changing our life conditions is about acknowledging where we trip ourselves up, picking ourselves up, dusting ourselves off and recommitting to the vision of how life can and should be.

Let me give you an example that's personal to me. 87 days ago, I promised myself I'd make time to write this book and complete a first draft in 90 days. In the first 84 days, I had managed to write just over 16,000 words. With the average book being about 50,000 words, this meant I was a little over 32% complete with my book. My inclination was to let myself off the hook and extend my deadline by another 60 days.

Monday morning at 6:15am, my coach invited me to a new possibility. "What if you stretched yourself and made it happen in the timeline you gave yourself?"

And just like that, the giant within me (I call him UnstoppaBILL) awoke, rubbed his eyes and recommitted to this project.

You know what happened? In just 48 hours, I produced an additional 21,000 words. And 72 hours in, I'm in the home stretch. I'm confident that the first draft of this book will be complete, in excellence, within the 90 days I gave myself. I changed my life conditions. I removed the obstacles, and I surprised myself in my ability to just be in the flow of the process that allowed me to complete this draft. As I write this, I have zero doubt I will accomplish what seemed impossible only two days ago. And, more importantly, I'm smiling the entire time I'm writing this, because I'm truly happy to share what I have kept inside me far too long.

Changing our blueprint is the other way to go. In the example above, I could have just as easily reset my expectations and been just as happy to finish the first draft of this book 60 days from now. Changing your blueprint is about being crystal clear about your expectations for how life is supposed to be and then taking a hard look at whether those expectations truly serve you.

During Tony Robbins' conference *Date with Destiny,* I discovered my primary question (the question I ask most often of myself) was "Why am I not successful?"

The blueprint I created for myself solidified and all but guaranteed that I would never be enough. It didn't matter how many awards I received, how much money I had in the bank, how many multi-million dollar companies I built from scratch and successfully exited. None of that mattered because my blueprint for success was virtually unattainable.

I compared myself to the likes of Sir Richard Branson and Tony Robbins himself and felt shitty. Talk about suffering. My blueprint was ridiculous, and I never stopped to question it. I felt I was in survival mode since age 12, when my dad walked out of our house. Worse, I felt that if I didn't become ridiculously successful, I'd either die or not be worthy of love. Letting go of that blueprint allowed me to create a brand new one that ensures I win every moment of every day. My new primary question is, "How can I appreciate this and make it even better?"

Let me answer that right now. I appreciate the opportunity to share what I've learned, and I will make it better by stopping here and sharing some of the other Tony Robbins success formulas that will serve you.

Tony Robbins' Formula for Contribution and the Art of Fulfillment

Perhaps my most favorite Tony Robbins quote (and I have many of them) is "The Secret to Living Is Giving." Phew. Mic drop moment. Let's unpack that as this formula itself will deliver so much happiness into your life.

When you give unconditionally of yourself, you make the world better in some meaningful way. When I serve my Unitarian Universalist Congregation at Shelter Rock youth group, I make a contribution to my local high school youth. When we then, collectively, decide to fill six vehicles full of food, clothing, and toiletries and head to New York City as part of a Midnight Run, we are supporting our local homeless with a combination of love and connection as well as the supplies they need. And when we give to anyone who needs our support, we provide fuel for life to flourish.

"The secret to living is giving."

A life that only supports you is not much of a life. Your impact on the world is marginal. Tony Robbins makes a distinction between "The Science of Achievement and the Art of Fulfillment." In other words, do you focus on being "Best IN the World" or "Best FOR the World?"

I spent the better part of my 20s and 30s racing to be "Best IN the World" only to discover in my 40s that true happiness comes from being "Best FOR the World." I made sweeping changes in my life and have honestly never been happier. I no longer experience the kind of stress I used to have every waking hour (and even when trying to get some rest). What's more, the moment I began focusing on how to be "Best FOR the World," I placed my needs for love and connection and contribution above my previous desire for certainty and significance. This was part of Tony Robbins Six Human Needs exercise at my very first *Unleash the Power Within* event, and it brought tremendous clarity and focus to my life.

The more we contribute to our communities and society at large, the more we see we are not living in scarcity at all. Abundance is all around us. We simply need to look and see what's right in front of us. Why is giving the secret to living? Because when you give completely and with no expectation of return, you feel fully alive.

Ray Dalio's Struggle Well

If you haven't already read the book *Principles* by Ray Dalio, don't let the number of pages deter you. According to Wikipedia, "Raymond Dalio is an American billionaire investor, a hedge fund manager, and philanthropist. Dalio is the founder of investment firm Bridgewater Associates, one of the world's largest hedge funds. Bloomberg ranked him as the world's 58th wealthiest person in June 2019."[25]

In his book, Ray Dalio talks about how happiness and struggle are intertwined. At first, I didn't get it. I thought happiness was the absence of struggle, but that's where I was wrong. Too much struggle, he argues, throws you into overwhelm where you feel defeated. But too little struggle is also a problem. And he should know. As the 58th wealthiest person, he could surely choose *not* to struggle if desired. With that kind of wealth, you could pay anyone to do just about anything and simply be.

Sounds wonderful until you think it through. After the massive binge watch on Netflix and eating orgy, then what? Travel around the world? Dance? Play? Sure, we can do many things to fill our time and just be a playboy equivalent. But I can see how, eventually, that would get old. Not enough struggle and boredom sets in. Happiness is not being bored out of your mind.

I see this in my kids during the summertime. After all the summer reading, homework and chores are done, they have endless amounts of screen time and play dates. And then they come to Elena and me and tell us they are bored. We, on the other hand, would LOVE to feel that way sometimes. With all the hustle and bustle of life, rarely do we experience the sensation of boredom. But that's what too little struggle feels like.

Struggling well is finding the peak balance between too much struggle, where you experience being overwhelmed, and too little struggle where you experience boredom. According to Ray Dalio this is where true happiness resides and why in our US Declaration of Independence it says, "Life, Liberty and the **pursuit** of Happiness." The pursuit gives life meaning and purpose. Finding a balance in our struggles will create the kind of happiness we seek.

Tal Ben-Shahar's Gratitude Formula

Perhaps you love these concepts but are looking for a definitive action plan you can start on tomorrow. If that's you, then let's dig into Dr. Tal Ben-Shahar's book *Happier*. "The backbone of the most popular course at Harvard," according to Martin Seligman, the author of *Authentic Happiness*.[26] He provides all sorts of exercises and tools in *Happier* – what I consider to be the definitive book on the subject of happiness.

One exercise, however, I can personally attest to will make a significant impact should you choose to implement it today. *Keep a Gratitude Journal and write down five things you are*

truly grateful for each day.

That's it. There are several relatively inexpensive gratitude journals you can buy on Amazon and have shipped to your house immediately (with free two-day shipping for Prime Members), but you don't actually need one. While having a dedicated journal can help some people, you don't need anything more than a piece of paper and a pen to get started.

In this moment as I'm writing, here are five things I'm truly grateful for right now:

1. I am grateful for you reading my book. Without you, there's no point in taking the time to write any of this down.

2. I am grateful that I have a coach who holds me to a high standard and challenges me to be the best version of myself (including writing this book).

3. I am grateful for my wife Elena who has continued to support me as I write and has contributed to the writing of this book.

4. I am grateful for my son Will (15 years old) whom, right now, is a CIT (counselor in training) supporting other kids enjoying Taekwondo camp.

5. I am grateful for my son Ryan (12 years old) who reminds me not to take life so seriously all the time and that I really should play more games with him.

And just like that, I'm a little bit happier than when I started writing. It so easy anyone can do it. In fact, you don't even need a pen or paper! Just take a moment, close your eyes and pick five things you're grateful for right now.

Go ahead. This book will still be here when you pick it back up. You're going to want to do this so you can see what I mean about changing your emotional state.

If you did stop reading, then you just experienced what I mean. **Gratitude shifts our attitude.** Even if you're seething mad and want to strangle someone, just close your eyes, take a deep breath and choose to find five things you're grateful for in that moment. You will experience a shift from one of anger to one of calm – and perhaps even some happiness and joy (depending on how fast you choose to shift your emotions).

According to Dr. Tal Ben-Shahar in his book *Happier,* "In research done by Robert Emmons and Michael McCullough, those who kept a daily gratitude journal – writing down at least five things for which they were grateful – enjoyed higher levels of emotional and physical well-being."[27]

Dr. Tal Ben-Shahar also sparked the weekend gratitude my family practices every week. As mentioned previously in the book, we all share three things we're grateful for before allowances are distributed. It's also a great anchor to associate gratitude with wealth. Elena and I have been doing this since our boys were toddlers, so this is all they've ever known when it comes to allowance.

As a side note, we also (sneakily) incorporated another happiness principle from Tony Robbins in that each of our kids receive allowances that are divisible by three. (1) Spending, (2) Saving, and (3) Giving. They each have three piles of cash. They deposit the savings into their bank account, can use their spending money any way they wish and choose which charities they want to make a contribution to. Since "the secret to living is giving," we thought we'd throw that in there too.

Trained psychological experts will have to tell us if it's better or worse for kids growing up with two certified coaches as parents and one of them a skilled trainer in transformation. (I can already see my son's eyes roll ;-)

Tony Hsieh's Purpose & Passion

I have a bromance with Tony Hsieh (he just doesn't know it). In case you can't place that name, Tony Hsieh is the CEO of Zappos and the author of *Delivering Happiness*. Another amazing book on the subject of happiness with an important and powerful distinction— it's about happiness at work.

Tony Hsieh's Happiness Framework #1 has four parts. (1) Perceived Control (2) Perceived Progress (3) Connectedness and (4) Vision/Meaning: Being part of something bigger than yourself. At work, this roughly breaks down to the levels of happiness you are likely to experience.

When you perceive you have control over your job, you have a good foundation for happiness. That is, when you know what's expected of you, the timeframe in which you are expected to perform and you believe you can accomplish the tasks you are given, you have perceived control over your job. Contrast that with a crazy boss who constantly wreaks havoc by changing priorities on a whim, giving you outrageous tasks with little to no time to complete them and expects you to answer texts and phone calls 24x7. It's a lot harder to maintain your happiness at work in that environment.

Perceived progress is the notion that you're being recognized for the growth in your job. From titles to responsibilities and pay, as you keep moving up the corporate ladder, you have a sense of satisfaction that the work you're doing means something to the company you work for. As you progress and receive recognition for the great work you're doing, you feel happy about the continued progress you're making throughout your career.

Connectedness is where Zappos shines. In his book, Tony Hsieh references Jonathan Haidt's book *The Happiness Hypothesis* and the idea that "happiness doesn't come primarily from within but, rather, from between. This is one of the reasons why we place so much emphasis on company culture at Zappos."[28] In other words, when you feel connected to the people you work with, you are happier at work. Sure, you may not feel 100% every day, but when you know there are people you respect who are counting on you, you feel connected, and that supports your longer-term happiness when working.

And finally, vision and meaning is one of the sustained hot topics in the business world, highlighted in books from Jim Collin's *Good to Great* to more recent authors like Simon Sinek, *Start with Why*. For Tony Hsieh, having a higher purpose that gives meaning to the work the company does is not only good for serving up higher levels of happiness at work, it also separates a great company from a good one. In essence, there's an argument to be made that being number one in a market has a lot to do with the vision and meaning that goes well beyond the day-to-day job requirements and that leads to higher profits as well as happier employees.

Tony Hsieh provides other business frameworks for delivering happiness, but **Happiness Framework #3** particularly captured my attention. For this framework, there are three parts. (1) Pleasure (2) Passion and (3) Higher Purpose. When it comes to understanding the formula for happiness this one sums it up nicely.

Pleasure seeking amounts to chasing happiness that is rooted in short-lived peaks. Think rock stars once they make it big. Sex, drugs and rock-and-roll all deliver short-term pleasure that doesn't last and isn't sustainable. Like a drug addict, pleasure-based happiness is only as good as the last bump you experienced. The new car bump is amazing for the first few days, and then it becomes the new normal and you stop appreciating it. A job promotion bump is great and after a few days, the pleasure from the promotion peters out. You get the idea.

Passion-based happiness is when you are "in the zone," and time ceases to exist. If you want to know what you are most passionate about, think back to the last time you were so engaged in what you were doing, time felt like it stopped. For example, when I'm downhill skiing, I'm so laser and present that time ceases to exist. When I'm writing so fast I feel the words flowing through my fingertips without the least bit of struggle. Or when I'm sparing a partner during a karate match, I may be aware of when I get tired, but I have no sense of time while I'm sparing. These are all examples of what Ray Dalio means when he wants us to "struggle well." It's the perfect balance of the right amount of challenge intersecting with your current skill level. Magic happens here.

For the third and final level, Tony Hsieh says, "The higher-purpose type of happiness is about being part of something bigger than yourself that has meaning to you. Research has shown that of the three types of happiness, this is the longest lasting."[29] That could be the causes you volunteer for or the children you care for. When you feel connected to something bigger than yourself, your happiness is rooted in the larger mission rather than your individual needs. This happiness lasts longer because you feel deeply connected to a purpose that is near and dear to your heart.

John C. Bogle: Stop Chasing the Rabbit

John C. Bogle is the founder of Vanguard Mutual Funds and, according to Wikipedia, he is credited with creating the first index fund. He wrote several books on investing, including *Enough: True Measures of Money, Business and Life*. In this book, he shares a story from the Reverend Fred Craddock who struck up a conversation with a retired greyhound:

I said to the dog, "Are you still racing?"

"No," he replied.

"Well, what was the matter? Did you get too old to race?"

"No, I still had some race in me."

"Well, what then? Did you not win?"

"I won over a million dollars for my owner."

"Well, what was it? Bad treatment?"

"Oh, no," the dog said. "They treated us royally when we were racing."

"Did you get crippled?"

"No."

"Then why?" I pressed. "Why?"

The dog answered, "I quit."

"You quit?"

"Yes," he said. "I quit."

"Why did you quit?"

"I just quit because after all that running and running and running, I found out that the rabbit I was chasing wasn't even real."[30]

What I love about the late John C. Bogle, including this in his book, is that he was arguably one of the most successful men on Wall Street, questioning if what we're all chasing is even real. How many people live their entire life in the proverbial "Rat Race" only to get to the tail end of their life and realize that what they deemed most important (i.e. "winning" and "getting ahead") was just a made-up construct?

He goes on to say it directly in his own words. "We'll be better human beings and achieve greater things if we challenge ourselves to pursue careers that create value for our society – with personal wealth not as the goal, but as the by-product. Best of all, by setting that challenge for ourselves, we'll build the character that will sustain us in our labors."[31] His perspective is that chasing the *real* rabbit of life is about serving our fellow men and women – not chasing wealth as the end goal.

Any of your friends who are financial advisors will know who John C. Bogle is and what Vanguard index funds are. While he certainly brought powerful financial instruments to the world, at the end of his life, John C. Bogle recognized that the formula for true happiness was being of service to our fellow humans.

The minute we get out of our heads and drop into our hearts, it's easy to reconnect with the happiness we seek. Happiness is being grateful for what we have (the essence of Enough) and seeing the abundance all around us. Being of contribution to those around us gives our life meaning and purpose, which keeps us on the path of sustained happiness.

SO WHAT? NOW WHAT?

A s I write this book, I'm coming off a 90-day journey called Living Integration[32] that was created by Altru Center: A Community for Altruistic Living. While I have had some of the most powerful experiences as part of this community, a simple and powerful concept was shared with me called, "So what, now what?" This concept contains three distinct questions: (1) What? (2) So what? And (3) Now what?

This is an opportunity for deep reflection.

When you apply this principle to marriage, it's one hell of a gift to give yourself. You have a choice here. You can blow through the remaining pages as an intellectual exercise, or use this section of the book to build your go-forward plan.

What?

Start here. Below are a series of questions to support you in figuring out what is currently going on in your marriage. These "what" questions are not intended for you to judge yourself or pick up the beat-up stick and start punishing yourself for the mistakes of the past. You can't change the past. The purpose of the questions in this section is to bring you clarity, nothing more.

If you want to make changes in your life, you first need clarity around where you are. Then (and only then) can you figure out where you want to go and how best to get there. Mapping out where you want to go is only as powerful as knowing where you truly are so you may plan for your migration from point A to point B.

Look at the questions below and pick the ones that jump out at you as a means to reflect and journal a bit about the current state of your marriage.

1. What happened?

2. What caused it? What led up to it?

3. What else have you observed in your marriage?

4. What was your part in this?

5. What is the biggest issue you'd like to resolve?

6. What were your expectations going into this marriage?

7. What hasn't lived up to your expectations?

8. What would need to change in order to have the marriage you desire?

9. What is your partner's primary love language?

10. In what ways have you used your partner's primary love language to deepen the quality of your marriage?

11. What is your primary love language?

12. How well does your partner know, understand and speak your primary love language?

13. When you are 95 years old, what will you want to say about your marriage?

14. How does your marriage relate to your life's purpose?

15. What part of your marriage, if any, are you unwilling to talk about?

16. What part of your marriage truly lights you up and you want to share with anyone and everyone who will listen?

17. In what ways are you fortunate to be married?

18. In what ways do you feel trapped or held back in your marriage?

19. When telling others what you love about your marriage, what do you share?

20. What sins has your partner committed that you either keep to yourself or share privately with your closest circle of confidants?

Be with these questions and write down what is coming up for you so you have a foundation from which to work. Your thoughts can go all over the place when they are unstructured, so take some time to think about the questions that support your deeper exploration of your marriage, and write down your answers. You never have to share this information with anyone and you are free to destroy these answers when you're done with the exercise.

So What?

Once you've captured the history of your marriage thus far, it's time to dig into the meaning you give it. These questions will support you in probing and a deeper exploration of what you just experienced in capturing different aspects of your marriage. It will also support you in creating a vision for how you'd like your marriage to be going forward.

1. How is your experience of being married different than what you expected?

2. How do you see (view) your marriage today?

3. What do you love about being married?

4. What do you dislike about being married?

5. What are some pressing needs in your marriage?

6. What part of your marriage has been an eye-opening experience?

7. What are some roles you play now in your marriage that you were not expecting to play?

8. How has your view of marriage changed?

9. How has being married affected you?

10. What did you do that seemed to work well in your marriage?

11. How has your experience of marriage affected the way you view your life?

12. What has surprised you about your marriage?

13. How has your understanding of marriage changed?

14. What have you learned from your experience of marriage?

15. How has your marriage changed you?

16. Who have you become in this marriage?

17. What is your most valuable lesson (with respect to your marriage)?

18. What do you now see as possible?

19. Where will this lead?

20. What is stopping you?

Now What?

Here's where the magic happens. You get to decide what actions you are committed to taking in order to have the marriage you desire. Leveraging the insights from the "What?" and "So What?" we can explore what you get to add in your marriage so you can design the marriage you can't wait to come home to each day.

1. What insights do you now have on your marriage? How will you apply them?

2. What would you like to stop happening or start happening in your marriage?

3. What aspects of your marriage do you wish to explore deeper with your partner?

4. What changes are you committed to making? By when?

5. If you could do this over, what changes would you make in your marriage?

6. How has your life expanded due to your marriage?

7. How can you continue to improve your marriage?

8. What are the possibilities?

9. What new options can you create?

10. If tomorrow you had the marriage of your dreams, what would be different?

11. What is your desired outcome?

12. How will you know you have reached it?

13. Who do you get to be in order to build the marriage you desire?

14. In what ways would you like to see change in your marriage?

15. Where do you go from here?

16. What resources will support you in building the marriage you want?

17. What part of your marriage have you not yet explored?

18. What aspects of your marriage are you most grateful for?

19. How will you pull all of these insights together?

20. What changes would your spouse need to see in order to be enrolled into this new vision for your marriage?

Just by reading this book, you've already taken the first step in supporting the long-term growth of your marriage. When you adhere to the Three Rules of Marriage, you will ensure that you and your spouse stay present with each other. By asking the important questions that support you and your partner, you can learn how to evolve from where you are today to where you'd like to be in the future.

The questions, "What? So what? Now what?" are designed to support you in not getting stuck. Your marriage will continue to evolve. Change in your marriage is inevitable, but continued growth and new levels of depth take a concerted effort. Your focus on your marriage will reward you with the joy and happiness that come from a union directly connected to your mission, purpose and desired outcomes in life and in your partner's life.

KNOWING THE PATH VS. WALKING THE PATH

In the words of the great poet Morpheus from the movie *The Matrix*, "There is a difference between knowing the path and walking the path."[33] Knowing what to do in your marriage is vastly different from doing what your marriage requires on a day-to-day basis.

Your marriage today is a perfect reflection of what you put into it and what you are willing to tolerate. Here's a secret. You are not your results! And results don't lie. Huh?

Let's start with the easy one, "results don't lie." What you have created in your marriage is reflected back to you as the sum total of the marriage that currently exists. If you don't like what you see, then change it. You have that power. And so does your spouse.

When I say, "You are not your results," that means you (and your spouse) are separate from the results of your marriage. You two are the people whose choices impact the quality of your marriage. The results and you are not the same thing. In other words, don't wrap your identity into your marriage. Sure, your marriage is an important part of your life, but it is not you. When you separate yourself from your marriage, what's left are three discreet areas of focus. (1) You (2) Your Spouse and (3) Your Marriage.

Your marriage is a perfect reflection of what's happened up to now. You can't change the results of the past, but you have every opportunity to change the results you don't like. You and your partner are in control here. When you see something you don't like, it's up to you to improve it or remove it.

184

Walking the Path

Even with all the insights from this book, rest assured that you're definitely going to make more mistakes. It's inevitable because we're imperfect beings. Walking the path isn't about being perfect—it's about being deliberate and being intentional. Walking the path is going beyond the knowledge of what one "should" do and stepping into what needs doing. Period.

Taking Responsibility

When my son Ryan was in the fifth grade, I came in for parent-teach night and read a sign that said, "If it's to be, it's up to me." His teacher, Mr. Talbot, explained that part of the lesson of being a fifth grader is taking responsibility – for your studying, homework, and your learning.

There are many people in their 40s and beyond who are still wrestling with the principle of responsibility. Walking the path in your marriage is about taking responsibility for your desired results. While you may rely on your partner for certain aspects of your marriage, it's up to you to change the things you want to improve.

Be | Do | Have

Ontology is the philosophical study of being[34]. Most of us have it backward. We go to school and decide what we want to have. Then we work backward from our havingness to our beingness. It goes like this:

- When I have the marriage of my dreams, I will

- Do whatever it takes and

- Be happy, joyful and complete

It's no different in any aspect of our life. "When I have the corner office and the executive position in my job, I'll do things differently around here, and I'll be incredibly successful."

Turns out, all of that is backwards because this thinking is going in the wrong order: Have > Do > Be. The correct order (and the only true way to walk the path) is Be > Do > Have. And it looks like this:

- When I am **BEING** happy, joyful and complete, I

- **Do** whatever it takes in order to

- **Have** the marriage of my dreams

Walking the path in your marriage doesn't start with the having (or even the doing)—it starts with the being. So who do you get to be in your marriage in order to have the marriage you want?

Here are some ways of being to support you walking the path.

Happy	Joyful	Present	Open	Connected
Loving	Accepting	Understanding	Urgent	Caring
Forgiving	Nurturing	Playful	Brilliant	Inspirational

You get the idea. There are many ways of being. You get to choose how you show up every time you are in front of your spouse. Instead of choosing a non-helpful way of being such as anger, frustration, disconnected, needy, you can choose from a place of vision, growth and prosperity.

What's more, your beingness will drive your doingness. When I am happy, I want to dance with my wife. When I am loving, I want to hug and snuggle up on my wife. When I am accepting, I listen without prejudice. When I am playful, I turn the chores around the house into a game. When I am connected, I **do** whatever my wife needs at the moment.

I **do** all of these things so that Elena and I both can **have** the life of our dreams. So if you want to have a blissful marriage, start with who you get to **be** in order to **do** the things that lead you to **have** that blissful marriage.

YOU'RE NOT ALONE. ASK (THE RIGHT PERSON) FOR THE HELP YOU NEED

I grew up Catholic. One of the things that really bothered me was the concept of the *martyr*. In the religious context, a martyr was someone who was willing to die for his or her beliefs. I also found several psychological martyrs. A psychological martyr is someone who is willing to endure a great deal of suffering for a particular belief or principle.

There's no badge of honor for being a martyr in your marriage. If things aren't working for you, then seek support. There are several options to choose from ranging from seeking the advice and counsel of the happily married couples you know who seem to have their act together to professional marriage counselors trained in therapy.

Find the Right Person

Find someone who will listen without judgment or prejudice. When you start opening up, if you feel unsafe or feel that you're being judged, then you're opening up to the wrong person – regardless of how good they seem to have it.

Seek out the non-judgmental types who are willing to support you. There are plenty of people in your network willing to take a stand for your happiness in your marriage. The right person is willing to listen to you, hear you out and help you think through the best solutions.

Get Some Group Support

Marriage support groups and marriage enrichment groups are available both in person and online. Some couples prefer not to go the marriage-counseling route and find solace in group support with other married couples experiencing their own challenges. Just be sure to check the reviews first so you don't find yourself in a prolonged bitch session – that's no fun.

Talk to Your Minister, Rabbi or Priest

If you consider yourself a highly or somewhat religious person, there's no shame in confiding in your religious leaders. They went to divinity school in order to support their congregants. You need only ask for support. Set up a meeting and share your challenges. If they are unable to support you, they have access to multiple resources who can.

Don't Suffer In Silence

If things aren't working out in your marriage, the only poor decision is to take no action at all. Even if you're an introvert by nature, this is one area of your life you don't want to "wait and see" what happens. Designing your ideal marriage requires you to lean into it and figure out how to make it work for you. Don't wait until your marriage is so rocky that the only viable option is to exit out of it. Step up now so you can have the marriage you deserve. Action today will support you for years to come.

ARE YOU WILLING TO INVEST ONE OR MORE FOUR-DAY WEEKEND(S) FOR TOTAL TRANSFORMATION?

Are you a slowly peel the Band-Aid off your skin or rip that sucker right off kind of person? If you're ready to take your marriage to the next level and prefer a weekend warrior option, you have many to choose from. I pretty much avoided these transformational seminars until about five years ago when I saw my life hitting a plateau. Now I can't get enough of them.

The immersion experience is so powerful because you are "in it" for several hours each day during (typically) four days. Don't let the long hours deter you. When you're in one of these transformational seminars, time seems to dissipate and you're amazed at how much ground you cover in a (relatively) short amount of time. If you're ready to go deep, here are some powerful options to consider.

Tony Robbins Unleash the Power Within[35]

This one is the first transformational event I attended, and it started me on a powerful path that totally shifted the quality of my life. Tony Robbins has been onstage for more than 40 years. He's the master, and this is his "introduction to transformation" event. You cover a tremendous amount of ground in four days. Come in on a Thursday, leave on a Sunday. These events are happening all the time all over the world. Find one close to home or pick a destination you've always wanted to visit. If you want to go big in your relationship, you're also welcome to dive into the deep end of the pool with Tony Robbins' Date with Destiny.[36] This is Tony's personal favorite event and the subject of the Netflix special, *Tony Robbins: I'm Not Your Guru.* If you're curious, watch the documentary. It's powerful stuff and a good overview of what to expect at the event.

Altru Center: Part 1 "Opening Awareness"

After completing every workshop and training that Tony Robbins had to offer, my friend, Paula Jennings, invited me to check out a local transformation center in New York City. I am forever grateful she did. In Part 1, *Opening Awareness,* you spend four days on self-discovery. As their website reads, "Who are you, once you strip away the trappings of modern life? Which core beliefs further your goals, and which ones limit you? Through exercises, games, lectures, sharing, small group work and close-eyed visualization, students have an opportunity to experience how you respond or react to life. This awareness creates new possibilities, new choices and personal insight, which begins to clear a path to a purpose-driven life."[37]

What I particularly enjoyed about Altru is that a good 50% of the training is experiential. Rather than tell you things, you play games and experience how you show up under controlled conditions. Favorite insight: "How you do one thing can show you how you do everything." In other words, how we play these games is the same as how we play life. Once you know yourself, you get to choose how you want to be going forward.

A Whole Host of Marriage Workshops

Do a Google search for "marriage workshops." You'll see so many great options to choose from. I can't speak to any of these as I have yet to attend any of them. When looking at the formats, they are very clear about what they offer and what you can expect to receive from them. Ask around and find out who's attended the ones in your area.

EXCEPTIONAL READING LIST

Throughout this book, I've referenced a number of fantastic books where I have received fantastic advice and insights. In addition to these books, I wanted to share some resources around the areas where most marriages struggle.

At one point, I was writing for Inc.com and was on the short list of every major publisher. They sent me advanced copies of so many books, I couldn't keep up. But as I caught up on my library, I discovered so many powerful books I'd love to share the most relevant ones that might support you in different aspects of your marriage. For anything a couple might fight over, I've found some powerful books that could help provide some support.

Happiness

When you're looking to dig deeper into increasing your happiness, start with either of these two books.

- *Happier* by Tal Ben-Shahar, Ph.D.

- *Delivering Happiness* by Tony Hsieh

Money & Investing

You know all those vital life skills no one ever teaches you in school? Here are two books that will support you so you don't waste money on buying stuff you don't need and understand the difference between working with a financial advisor and a fiduciary (someone who is legally required to put your financial interests above their own).

- *Pogue's Basics: Money* by David Pogue

- *Money: Master the Game* by Tony Robbins

Career

Trying to figure out what career you should be in and/or how to get ahead in your current job? Try these on for size.

- *Bullshit Jobs* by David Graeber

- *Good to Great* by Jim Collins

- *7 Habits of Highly Effective People* by Steven Covey

Love

When it comes to understanding love, there are so many great books to choose from. These are my personal favorites, and the first is a MUST read for all married couples.

- *The Five Love Languages* by Gary Chapman

- *The Mastery of Love* by Don Miguel Ruiz

Life

What's the point? Why am I here? Does any of this stuff even matter? If these questions keep you up at night, check out these books.

- *Source Movement* by Jo Englesson

- *A New Earth: Awakening to Your Life's Purpose* by Eckhart Tolle

Vulnerability

There is one de facto expert on the topic of shame and vulnerability, and that's Brené Brown. You can't go wrong with any of her books, but I highly recommend starting with:

- *Daring Greatly: How the Courage to Be Vulnerable Transforms the Way We Live, Love, Parent, and Lead* by Brené Brown

Pregnant

If you're about to have your first child, it's a little freaky to think that there's no manual. The closest thing out there that will support you are these two amazing books.

- *What to Expect When You're Expecting* by Heidi Murkoff and Sharon Mazel

- *The Girlfriends Guide to Pregnancy* by Vicki Iovine

Parenting

If you're a new parent, life just got fascinating. The most overwhelming part of having a newborn is knowing what to buy from the thousands upon thousands of baby product options. Start here.

- *Baby Bargains: Your Baby Registry Cheat Sheet* by Denise & Alan Fields

- *Babywise: Giving Your Infant the Gift of Nighttime Sleep* by Robert Bucknam M.D.

Being a Man

Between emotional intelligence, #MeToo, Mansplaining and the general attack on all things masculine (hey, let's face it, us men had a good run), it's time for a rest on how to be a man – especially at the office. There may be others like it out there, but I'm a big fan of:

- *Future Man: How to Evolve and Thrive in the Age of Trump, Mansplainging, and #MeToo* by Tim Samuels

Starting and Running a Business

Let's face it—starting a business from scratch may be an American dream. But it's going to take just about everything you have to be successful. These books will drastically improve your odds of success.

- *Zero to One* by Peter Thiel

- *The Ultimate Sales Machine* by Chet Holmes

- *Rich Dad, Poor Dad* by Robert T. Kiyosaki

- *Secrets of the Millionaire Mind* by T. Harv Eker

- *The Million-Dollar One-Person Business* by Elaine Pofeldt

Retirement

This one is so much more important when you're in your 20s and 30s, but so few people start as early as they need to. Please, for your own sake, prioritize reading these books to ensure you retire wealthy.

- *Unshakable* by Tony Robbins

- *Be Your Best Boss* by William Seagraves

Powerful Self-Improvement

When the focus is on how to be better, live better and take

yourself to the next level, this is where you want to start.

- *Principles: Live and Work* by Ray Dalio

- *Unlimited Power: The New Science of Personal Achievement* by Tony Robbins

- *The Difference* by Subir Chowdhury

Time Management

Regardless of whether at home or at work, managing your time is one of the most important things you can do to maximize your desired outcomes. There are lots of books on this subject, and here are my favorites.

- *Time Isn't the Problem: Four Strategies to Transform Stress Into Success* by Chad E. Cooper

- The 4-Hour Workweek: Escape 9-5, Live Anywhere and Join the New Rich *by Timothy Ferriss*

Success

While many of the books already mentioned will support your drive toward success, there are two books in particular that hit the nail on the proverbial head.

- *The 7 Spiritual Laws of Success* by Deepak Chopra

- *The 4 Agreements* by Don Miguel Ruiz

Why Everything is Fucked

And when all else fails, turn to Mark Manson for his brilliant insights on why everything is fucked and how not to give one.

- *Everything is Fucked: A Book About Hope* by Mark Manson

- *The Subtle Art of Not Giving a Fuck: A Counterintuitive Approach to Living a Good Life* by Mark Manson

Sex

While still on the topic, there are SO many great books about sex, it really depends what you're in to. I urge you to explore fetishes, kinks and all the stuff you're even mildly curious about. Sex is so important in the marriage. I want to acknowledge that my wife loves to listen to the *Savage Lovecast* – a powerful podcast about sex by Dan Savage. I'm partial to PornHub. What does that tell you? Guys are more visual learners and women are more auditory learners.

END NOTES

[1] "III Sides to Every Story." (2020, May 19). In *Wikipedia* retrieved from https://en.wikipedia.org/wiki/III_Sides_to_Every_Story

[2] American Psychological Association. (2020, May 21). "Marriage & Divorce." Adapted from the Encyclopedia of Psychology. https://www.apa.org/topics/divorce/

[3] Oxford Dictionary. (Accessed May 19, 2020). https://www.lexico.com/en/definition/stoic

[4] "Stoicism." (2020, May 19). In *Wikipedia* retrieved from https://en.wikipedia.org/wiki/Stoicism

[5] Eker, T. Harv. *Secrets of the Millionaire Mind*. HarperCollins. ©2005. page 169

[6] "Career Leaders & Records for Batting Average." (2020, May 27). Baseball Reference. https://www.baseball-reference.com/leaders/batting_avg_career.shtml

[7] "Happier People Live Longer Lives." (Accessed June 3, 2020). https://www.telegraph.co.uk/news/health/news/8860123/Happier-people-live-longer-lives.html

[8] Fierer, Lisa. "What Is Kundalini Yoga?" (2020, January 3). https://www.gaia.com/article/what-is-kundalini-yoga

[9] Speaker, Kyle MacDonald. (2015, November 20). "What If..." [Video File]. Retrieved from https://www.youtube.com/watch?v=8s3bdVxuFBs

[10] Devon Ivie. "*SNL*'s Brutally Honest Tour Guide Wants to Temper Vacation Expectations For You". (2019, May 5) https://www.vulture.com/2019/05/snl-adam-sandler-is-a-brutally-honest-italian-tour-guide.html

[11] "Conscious Camping-Tantra Week." (Accessed May 5, 2020). Ängsbacka https://www.angsbacka.se/en/event/tantra-festival/

[12] Unitarian Universalist Congregation at Shelter Rock. (Accessed May 16, 2020). https://uucsr.org/

[13] Eckhart Tolle. *A New Earth: Awakening to Your Life's Purpose.* Penguin. 2008. https://www.amazon.com/New-Earth-Awakening-Purpose-Selection/dp/0452289963

[14] ALTRU Center: A Community for Altruistic Living. https://www.altrucenter.org/workshops

[15] www.headphonedisco.com/silent-disco-headphones/

[16] Noom. https://friends.noom.com/YVFRWFVJOFpaOmNm

[17] Batterson, *Mark. In a Pit with a Lion on a Snowy Day: How to Survive and Thrive When Opportunity Roars.* Multnomah Books. ©2006. Quote retrieved from Good Reads https://www.goodreads.com/quotes/1834670-even-choosing-to-do-nothing-is-still-making-a-choice

[18] Carmody, Bill. Tony Robbins Interview Part I. YouTube. September 11 ,2016. https://www.youtube.com/watch?v=yT0eDgWdNts&list=PLdonwru96NY3B3vUhEa22APumkfA-cFzb

[19] Vinciguerr, Thomas. "A Bundle of Joy Isn't Enough?" The New York Times. (December 6, 2007). https://www.nytimes.com/2007/12/06/fashion/06push.html

[20] Bobby, Dr. Lisa Marie. "Marriage Counseling Questions- How To Find a (Good!) Marriage Counselor". Growing Self. https://www.growingself.com/marriage-counseling-denver/marriage-counseling-questions/how-to-choose-a-marriage-counselor/

[21] Ibid

[22] Maguire, Emer. (2015, March 11) "What's in a kiss? The science of smooching." https://www.britishcouncil.org/voices-magazine/kiss-science-smooching

[23] Samuels, Tim. *Future Man: How to Evolve and Thrive In the Age of Trump, Mansplaining, and #Metoo.* Arcade Publishing. © 2019. page 39.

[24] The American College of Obstetrics and Gynecologists. https://www.acog.org/patient-resources/faqs/gynecologic-problems/disorders-of-the-vulva-common-causes-of-vulvar-pain-burning-and-itching

[25] "Ray Dalio." (2020, May 7). In *Wikipedia* retrieved from https://en.wikipedia.org/wiki/Ray_Dalio

[26] Ben-Shahar, Ph.D., Tal. *Happier.* McGraw Hill ©2007, page x.

[27] Ibid, page 10.

[28] Hsieh, Tony. *Delivering Happiness: A Path to Profits, Passion and Purpose.* Hachette Book Group. ©2010, page 234.

[29] Ibid, page 237.

[30] Bogle, John C. *Enough: True Measures of Money, Business and Life.* John Wiley & Sons. ©2009. pages 211-212.

[31] Ibid, page 224.

[32] ALTRU Center: A Community for Altruistic Living. https://www.altrucenter.org/workshops

[33] Silver, J. (Producer) & Wachowski, L., & Wachowski, L. (Directors). (1999). *The Matrix*. [Motion Picture]. United States. Warner Bros.

[34] Ontology. (2020, May 21). In *Wikipedia* retrieved from https://en.wikipedia.org/wiki/Ontology

[35] Robins, Tony. Unleash the Power Within. (Accessed May 19, 2020). https://www.tonyrobbins.com/events/unleash-the-power-within/

[36] Robbins, Tony. Date with Destiny. (Accessed May 19, 2020). https://www.tonyrobbins.com/events/date-with-destiny/

[37] ALTRU Center: A Community for Altruistic Living. https://www.altrucenter.org/workshops

ACKNOWLEDGMENTS

I really appreciate Elena co-writing this book with me. I know I tend to be the voice that carries in this book. But Elena has been my voice of reason for the past 20 years. I love it when she is passionate about any subject, and this one is near and dear to me. Recently I heard the quote, "If you want to go fast, go alone. If you want to go far, engage your team." Elena is the most valuable player (MVP) on our team. I am who I am because of the love and support she has given me. I trust that her words provide some key insights about who we are as a couple and how we choose to be in our relationship with each other.

To my boys, Will and Ryan, thank you for being my greatest teachers. Raising each of you has given me a deep sense of purpose and an opportunity to be a better man, father and husband to Elena. Each of you inspires me to be better every day and reflect back the values and principles I hold dear in our family.

Mom (Mary Jo Carmody), Dad (William J Carmody, Sr.) and Step-Mom (Georgiana Carmody), without the three of you, I would never have believed in the healing power of love after a divorce. To watch the three of you interact with each other gives me hope for so many of my friends who are divorced (or in the process of getting a divorce). You are a beautiful model of how things can be. Thank you for being such fantastic model parents. My kids are benefiting from your parental examples.

To Connie & Richard Knies, your incredible 64-year marriage was the inspiration for this book. It was, after all, your rules that inspired me to create a blissful marriage and then share what has worked with anyone who will listen.

Brian Carmody, I'm lucky to have a brother like you. Thank you for all your keen insights and perspective on marriage. You challenged me to be clear on what I want in my marriage, to be vocal about it with Elena and to never harbor negative emotions. I'm really lucky to have an enlightened man who is also my brother.

Merrit & Carrol Maddux, your wedding in Hong Kong is the reason I became a world traveler. Having you as an older step-brother later in life, Merrit, was such an incredible gift I wasn't expecting after my dad married your mom. Mitch Maddux, I appreciate all the weekend get-togethers in Montclair, NJ as I was growing up. Michelle Maddux-Klippert, your love for the late Kyle Klippert showed me just how deep love can grow in a marriage.

I'd like to thank all of my coaching clients who inspired me to go deep on the subject of marriage for this book. While I tend to focus on the business side of coaching, it's clear just how much of an impact a happy (or conversely, an unhappy) marriage makes on any business. You have challenged me to go deep here and I'm better because of my opportunity to work with each of you. Thank you!

Thank you to Tony Robbins and his massive team of volunteer Trainers and Senior Leaders who challenged me to be my best self and take my relationship as far as it could possibly go. Special thanks to Chad Cooper, my very first executive coach and long-time friend who challenged and inspired me to become a coach and trainer.

Speaking of becoming the best person I can be, I want to thank

Bettie J. Spruill, Francine Rahe, Chis Austin, Kris Delgado, and Michael Desanti for showing me what being best FOR the world looks like as a trainer. And to Tonya Parris and the Altru Center generators, captains and coaches who challenged me to continue to take my life to the next level and inspired me to write the bulk of this book during my Part 3 (Living Integration) 90-day period. When I commit to my commitments, magic and this book happen in the world.

In addition to my coaching work, I had the time and inclination to write this book because I was supported by three incredible individuals. Tracey McCormack, thank you for giving me the opportunity to collaborate with you as a trainer. I appreciate your guidance, support and continued partnership. I have learned so much from you. Maria Weicker, you are an incredible client and Publics Media is lucky to have you. Likewise, Karen Erasmus you are powerful leader and MediaCom is a better company because of all of your efforts.

Thank you Shirzad Chamine for inviting me into your company, Positive Intelligence. Your 6-week program has had a profound impact on my day-to-day happiness, including weakening my saboteurs and strengthen my sage and self-command muscles. Your mental fitness work has supported me in the continuous growth of my marriage and family dynamic.

Jenn T. Grace, the brilliance of your "Getting Started for Authors Blueprint" was only matched by your selfless generosity of introducing me to Halo Publishing. Lisa Umina, thank you for how clear, easy and straightforward you made it to publish this book. And Lisa Bell, all of your edits has made this book so much better than what I originally wrote. Brooke W. Cooper, thank you for proofing this book. Your command of language and grammar is so impressive. Any errors are my own. And Donald Allen, it's no wonder you're a best-selling author. Your suggestions to add more punch in this book showed me what was in my blind spot. Thanks for your incredible feedback.

And thank you, my reader, for taking the time to read (or listen to) this book. Without you, I'm just talking to myself. Even if we've never met in person, it is ultimately because of you and your willingness to read this book, that I wrote it in the first place. I am, because you are.

ABOUT BILL CARMODY

B ill Carmody is a TEDx Storyteller, author and a Professional Certified Coach (PCC) with the International Coaching Federation (ICF). When he is not supporting his clients and dear friends in their relationships and careers, he delivers powerful week-long trainings for marketing and media companies such as WPP and Publicis Media. Bill founded two multi-million dollar award-winning marketing agencies, one when he first got married and the second after the birth of his second child. As an international keynote speaker and former contributing writer for Inc.com, Bill had the honor and privilege to interview celebrities such as Tony Robbins and Sir Richard Branson. Bill also had the distinct honor of supporting the public speaking training skills for members of the Brexit team. If you would like to know more about him, please connect with Bill on LinkedIn or follow him on Twitter @BillCarmody. For your free 1-hour coaching session, go to BillCarmody.com/coaching for details.

ABOUT ELENA CARMODY

E lena Carmody is a Certified Leadership Coach having completed her training with Coach 4 Life. In addition to working at several award-winning marketing agencies, she has been belly dancing for nearly 20 years. Elena runs a tight ship at the Carmody household, overseeing the finances, food and cleanliness. Her sons Will and Ryan concur that Elena is the glue that holds the family unit together. While their dad (Bill) may have the fun jobs, Elena has found a balance between disciplinarian and chief nurturer. Elena has powerful experience of juggling the responsibilities of family life with career, vacation and marriage. In her down time (Ha! As if!) she enjoys painting, cross-stitch, reading and podcasts including *Savage Lovecast*.